It's Time To Go Up!

It's Time To Go Up!

Nico Smit

Copyright © 2025 by Nico Smit

nicosmitblog.com

First published by Yeshua Collective 2025
All rights reserved. No part of this book may be reproduced in any manner whatsoever without written permission except in the case of brief quotations embodied in critical articles and reviews.

Unless otherwise noted, all scriptures are from THE HOLY BIBLE, NEW INTERNATIONAL VERSION®. Copyright© 1973, 1978, 1984, 2011 by Biblica, Inc.™. Used by permission of Zondervan.

Scripture quotations marked (NKJV) are taken from the NEW KING JAMES VERSION®. Copyright© 1982 by Thomas Nelson, Inc. Used by permission. All rights reserved.

First Printing by Ingram Spark 2025
ISBN (print book): 9781763547636
ISBN (ebook): 9781763547643

Published by Yeshua Collective
58 Channel Highway, Kingston TAS 7050
PO Box 329, Kingston TAS 7051
yeshuacollective.com

Cover design by Matthew de Livera, @mdfilmcreative
Edited by BekkerMedia, New South Wales, Australia

CONTENTS

ENDORSEMENTS	vii
FOREWORD	xi
PROLOGUE	xiii

	Introduction	1
Part One - Intimacy And Worship		7
1	The Call To Come Closer	9
2	Living In His Presence	19
3	Worship As A Lifestyle	29
Part Two - The Power Of Prayer		43
4	Going Higher Through Prayer	47
5	The Prayer Of Intimacy	55
6	Intercession—Birthing Revival	61
Part Three - Revival		67
7	What is Revival?	69
8	The Role of Holiness in Revival	75
9	Revival Starts with You	81
	Conclusion: Stay Up Here	87

Endorsements

Long has our generation needed a reminder of what its role is in revival and its responsibility in the initiation of one. Too long, the Church has remained dormant and silent, passive and inactive when She is called to be the Light of the World, the City on a Hill, and the restraining force against the enemy. Pastor Nico, a real revivalist, a seasoned minister of real substance and a man after God's own heart, serves as an inspiration to us... and an example of the fruit of a life that is truly consecrated and ever hungry and thirsty for a move of God. May every reader be challenged, educated, encouraged and equipped to "Go Up", and may we all be "ruined for anything less than living continuously in the fullness of God's presence."

Thank you, Ps Nico for writing this as a call for the Church to awaken and be The Remnant in this hour!

Dr. Brad Norman, London UK, *Revival Ministries UK, Founder Salvation for the Nations, President RBI London, Director FaithUK TV*

Nico Smit is one of the most effective and innovative apostolic leaders I have met. I have seen the fruit of Nico's ministry, and he is gifted at encouraging and empowering people of all ages to step into revival.

Get ready to "Go Up" and intimately connect with your Father in Heaven! Get ready to surrender everything to Jesus and live from His unlimited presence! But be careful too; I know that if you read this book and do what it says, you will experience an outbreak of revival in your life and your world will never be the same!

Dave Harvey, Redding California USA, *Pastor at Bethel Church, Director at Bethel Leaders Network*

Nico Smit has penned the heart of God in his incredible book, *It's time to go Up*. This book is a gift and compass from the Lord releasing direction, revelation, clarity, invitation and insight for this unprecedented and important hour we are living in. As you read through these pages, you will be taken into deeper realms of intimacy with the Lord as revelation floods into your life, beckoning you higher and posturing you in clarity, for the mighty move of His Spirit we are going to see in the earth.

Full of wisdom and His strategy to arm you for the days ahead, this book will leave you hungering with deeper desperation for Jesus, co-labouring with Him in seeing the Kingdom of God advanced and living from your seat as an overcomer. It's time to go up!

Lana Vawser, Sydney Australia, *Author and Prophet, Lana Vawser Ministries, Author of "The Prophetic Voice of God", "A time to Selah" and "I hear the Lord say New Era"*

Nico Smit's *It's Time To Go Up* is a profound and timely invitation to ascend into the fullness of God's presence, to live fully alive, and to partner with heaven for revival. With a deep passion for God, people, and the transformative power of intercession, Nico masterfully guides readers on a journey to exchange the fleeting high places of this world for the eternal, heavenly places in Him.

Drawing from decades of ministry experience across six continents, Nico brings a unique perspective that blends practical teaching, spiritual depth, and an undeniable passion for revival. In his chapter *Intercession—Birthing Revival*, he unpacks a powerful truth: every great move of God, from Pentecost to the Welsh Revival, was birthed in the prayer room. He reminds us that before revival can touch nations, it must first ignite in the hearts of believers willing to labour in persistent, fervent prayer. Revival, as Nico so brilliantly shares, is birthed in the secret place and sustained by a personal encounter with God.

This book is more than a call to action—it's a roadmap to a transformed life and a revived church. Nico's wisdom and passion challenges readers to go deeper, to see the world through God's eyes, and to embrace the cost of personal and corporate intercession. Whether you are a seasoned believer or seeking a fresh encounter with God, *It's Time To Go Up* will inspire, equip, and empower you to step into your God-given potential and partner with Him for revival in our time.

I wholeheartedly recommend this book to anyone longing to live with intentionality, see lives changed, and witness God move in power. Nico Smit's heart for revival, practical insight, and profound faith will leave you both challenged and encouraged to ascend higher into the presence of God and into the life you were created to live. This is not just a book; it's a call to transformation and a commissioning for every believer.

Daniel Hagen, Sunshine Coast Queensland Australia, *Lead Pastor Fire Churches Australia, Associate Director Awakening Australia | Awakening Music*

Pastor Nico Smit's book is a powerful invitation to experience God's presence in a deeper way. With profound theological insight and practical wisdom, he calls readers to deepen their relationship with God through worship, prayer, and personal revival. This book is a powerful guide for anyone seeking to live in the fullness of God's glory and experience lasting spiritual renewal. Pastor Nico's message is both inspiring and life changing.

Adnan Maqsood, Houston Texas USA, *Late-Night Talk Show Host, Televangelist, Preacher and Author, President Vision TV Networks, Founder of Vision Ministries International, General Manager at CTN (Christian Television Network)*

| X | -

Foreword

What a delight it is to introduce you to Nico Smit's *It's Time to Go Up!*—a treasure waiting to bless your heart and draw you closer to the Father. This book is a gentle yet powerful invitation to step into deeper intimacy with God and experience the abundant life that flows from walking closely with Him.

In the hustle and busyness of life, it's all too easy to feel swept up in the noise and distractions. Yet, deep within, there's a longing—a yearning for more, for the richness of God's presence. Nico beautifully speaks to that longing, reminding us that God is always calling us closer, beckoning us to lean into His love and discover the transformative joy of His fellowship.

Through the pages of this book, Nico tenderly guides us into the heart of prayer and worship—not as lifeless rituals but as vibrant, life-giving expressions of our connection with God. With heartfelt stories and practical insights, he shows how revival begins not in grand spectacles but within the quiet, surrendered moments when we choose to draw near to Him.

The truth Nico shares is refreshingly simple yet profoundly life-changing: your relationship with God matters. Your prayers, your worship, and your choice to cultivate intimacy with Him can ignite transformation—not only in your own life but in the lives of those around you. When you say "yes" to His invitation to go higher, you'll discover the incredible ways His love flows through you to touch your family, friends, and community.

As you journey through this book, may your heart be stirred to make space for God in fresh and meaningful ways. Let Nico's words inspire you to embrace a lifestyle of worship, to engage in heartfelt prayer, and to delight in walking hand in hand with your Creator. This journey isn't about striving; it's about enjoying His presence and letting His love transform every part of your life.

I pray that as you read, you will feel the gentle nudge of the Holy Spirit, drawing you closer to the One who loves you more than you can imagine. May you experience a renewed sense of purpose, a fresh awareness of His presence, and the unshakable joy that comes from knowing Him intimately.

Happy reading, dear friend! May this book be a sweet companion on your journey upward and closer to His heart.

With love,
Katherine Ruonala
Senior leader of Glory City Church in Brisbane, Australia
Overseer of the International Glory City Church Network
Founder and leader of Australian Prophetic Council
www.katherineruonala.com

Prologue

Revival lives in hungry prayers and thirsty worship!

I've heard people ask, "Where are the revivals?" and "Why are we not seeing greater moves of God?", but the same people often make very little room for passionate, intentional and desperate pursuits of God in their life. We constantly try to deflect responsibility for a move of God away from ourselves, but we are often the ones not making room and time for intimacy with God.

Who is holding back a move of God? Honestly, it's not God!!! He is willing! He is a loving heavenly Father who is drawn to the affections of His children.

I've discovered God loves talking to me, He eagerly desires to be close to me and He loves spending time with me! He is constantly calling me to come closer, to come higher and to come alive in His presence.

The most amazing evidence of God's desire to be with me is His Holy Spirit. He put His Holy Spirit in me so I will always have quick access into His presence. This is true for you too. God has set it up so that nobody would ever be too poor, too far, too weak, too busy or too burdened to worship and pray. God built something very special into humanity that can only be activated when His people humble themselves, seek His face and pray. People were created to SEEK THE LORD and be found by Him.

God has always said: "COME CLOSER! COME UP HERE! DRAW NEAR TO ME! LET US BE TOGETHER!" Right now, heaven is waiting for your response to God's invitation!

My story is both ordinary and extraordinary at the same time! At 23 years of age, I was born again in revival and that has ruined me for anything less than living continuously in the fullness of God's presence! As I draw near to Him there has always been a guarantee that He WILL draw near to me. Acts 3:19 states that times of refreshing (renewal and revival) come from the presence of the Lord. My experience was cemented in the reality that wherever God is everything must live in revival, because He is resurrection and life! It is not possible to have His life flowing through you and not be in revival.

Many of the pursuits of men are like chasing mirages in the dessert. From afar they look awesome, but when you get there, they are just empty, worthless and thirsty spaces. This was my life before I surrendered to God. At that time, it was clear to me that my life was messed up, I was not doing well, and sin had a strong hold on me. In early 1992 I was born again during a significant move of God in Durban, South Africa. I was not a Christian at the time and did not plan to become one, but somehow, one night, I found myself at a local church where God was so powerfully present that everything in me fell in love with Him. It was the realest thing I had ever experienced, and it set my heart on fire with a blaze I could not control and would never want to lose.

The blessing of the Christian life is found only in God. My human heart was looking for water that could revive it and power that could awaken it. What I found was the source of life and goodness itself. God invited me to follow Jesus into a place where my sin, my depravity, my addictions, my anger and my enemies could not go. I realized that even though I was born in sin, I was not created for sin. I was made for a much higher life. I had a choice to make. I could go up or I could remain as I was. I could remain in the state I was born in or become born-again into the purpose I was created for. I decided that I would never again be content to live any other way but in hot pursuit of God. Once I tasted the goodness of God, felt the warmth of His love and encountered the beauty of His power I knew there could never be a turning back for me.

Going up, for me, is not an option.

Going up is everything!

Although I have preached many messages, enjoyed many revivals, seen thousands saved, raised lots of Jesus followers, witnessed countless miracles and planted hundreds of churches around the world... this was never my primary goal, destination or reward. No, my greatest desire has always been to go where God goes, do what God is doing and never leave

His presence for any other pursuit. I decided that I can only be of any earthly good if I'm willing to be heavenly minded. This is the passion behind this book.

We were made for sacred places and the most sacred place of all is the heart of God. Nothing good can flow from setting my mind and heart on earthly things. God's supernatural womb is worship and prayer. That is where promises are formed, destinies are created, and blessings are prepared before they're birthed! The reality is... Nothing of any eternal value or earthly blessing will come but from these places. Going up in worship and prayer is the only way to stay spiritually in revival!

Are you wanting a true move of God? Then you must know: Revivals start at the worship altar in the prayer room. A great prayer life is always built on a great worship life. Revivals do not start without hunger and thirst. They do not start on our terms, but on God's. If your upper room commitment is real, then so shall your encounters be!

Revival is waiting for people who are willing to put their programs, agendas and comforts aside because all they want, need and desire is God and Him glorified! This is not religion or religious. This is a revelation that God wants intimacy and closeness with us. He wants sons and daughters, not mere employees or subscribers. Revival will never come to an upper room where God is not welcome.

Faith grows and victories accumulate when you talk to God.
Revival comes where people end, and God begins.
Revival is waiting for surrendered worshippers and committed prayers!

A.W. Tozer said: *The missing jewel in the church today is worship! There can be no faith without worshipping the faith-giver. Opening your mouth and filling it with adoration to God is the secret to strengthening faith and drawing nearer to Him.*

Introduction

God's call to humanity has always been, *"Come closer!"* expecting our response to echo back to Him… *"Yes, Lord, be it unto me according to your desire."* We are meant to be a people who live, move and have our whole being in a daily reality of the presence of God! We were made to be most effective, complete and content when we're in communion with Him. To live in Him is to be fully alive!

This truth cannot be overstated, because every day in this world we have so many things fighting for our attention, drawing our strength, demanding our commitment and breaking our hearts. Everything wants us to pay a price. It's not uncommon to feel like everything wants the high places of our hearts. Everything wants to rule and reign over our lives, but nothing seems to make sense or bring us true life.

The noise of this world wants us to forget God is a different kind of high place. He is a heavenly place. In an upside-down world where social distancing, separation, breakdown and isolation has become the norm, we have a God that breaks through all that noise with a personal invitation to relationship that never changes: *"Come up here! Come closer! I want to show you great and mighty things."*

From the very beginning of creation, there has been this deep, relentless invitation to mankind to draw near to God, to go beyond the surface, and to truly live in His presence. You must see, it has never been our Father that has kept people at arm's length. You will never hear Him say, *"Stand back! You're too close."* No, He has always been the One who calls us home with open arms. He has always been the One inviting us to ascend higher into Him so we can see things from His perspective. You cannot draw near to God and not find yourself ascending higher and deeper into the life you were created to live.

There is something very special about stepping up, moving out of your comfort zone, and seeing the world as God sees it. It is a journey well worth taking.

It's time to go up! It is time to exchange the high places of this world for the heavenly places in Him.

The Invitation to Come Closer

God's invitation is as personal as it is profound. *"Come closer,"* He says. Nobody has ever gotten too close to God. God has never said: "TOO CLOSE!" and you will never hear Him say: "LEAVE ME ALONE!" It is not possible to invade His personal space or to be unwelcome when you heed His call to come.

Just like Moses, who was called from the wilderness to the burning bush, we too are called to step up and come closer. You too have an invitation to a burning bush and holy ground. There is more. There is always more with God, more to see, more to experience, and more to understand. But you cannot see these things from where you are. There is a step up required.

When God calls us higher, it is not just to see things differently but to live differently. Jesus often called His disciples up to the mountain, away from the crowds, to reveal deeper truths. He waits for us to respond to His call, to ascend the mountain and sit at His feet. There, in His presence, we find clarity, peace, and a renewed sense of purpose.

The higher you go, the more you will be able to see. From the mountaintop, your vision changes. Everything comes into perspective, and you see things as they are. The things that once seemed overwhelming and impossible shrink in the light of God's glory. The struggles, the fears, the anxieties—they fade as you set your mind on things above where God is.

Consider Colossians 3:1-4 where Paul says, *"Since you have been raised with Christ, strive for the things above, where Christ is seated at the right hand of God. SET YOUR MINDS ON THINGS ABOVE, NOT ON EARTHLY THINGS. For you died, and your life is now hidden with Christ in God. When Christ, who is your life, appears, then you also will appear with Him in glory."* (Emphasis mine)

There's peace in knowing that God's perspective is so much greater than our own. And as you draw closer, you will find that your capacity to handle life's challenges increases. The further you can see, the further you can reach.

How do you set your mind? By worship, prayer and surrendering to His power in us!

Living in His Presence

There are no substitutes for living in the presence of God. Nothing - and I mean NOTHING - can fill the space in your life that's reserved for Him. You might try to fill it with other things—success, relationships, things, achievements—but only God's presence brings fullness of joy. As Psalm 16:11 (NKJV) says, *"In Your presence is fullness of joy; at Your right hand are pleasures forevermore."*

God's presence is not something you have to earn. It is something you can enter by faith, by choice. The door is always open if you want to step in. But it is up to you. You decide. You set the pace. When you draw near, He responds by also drawing near. When you abide so does He. You must make your dwelling place alongside Him. When you do, everything changes. Revival, renewal, and transformation flow from the presence of God.

Revival, in its simplest form, is becoming more aware of God's presence. It is when you realise that the Creator of the universe is right here, right now, moving in your life. His presence always causes change. You cannot encounter God and stay the same. The more you press into Him, the more you will see your life renewed, refreshed, and revived.

When you draw near to God, He changes you forever, for the better, because its not possible to draw near to God without that leading to you ascending to higher places in Him.

Ascending Higher in Worship and Prayer

Worship is the believer's ascent. It is more than a song, it's a life laid down, a heart surrendered to the King of kings. Worship brings you into the throne room, where you can see God for who He truly is—holy, glorious, wonderful, beautiful, powerful and deserving of all honour. But worship also reveals who we are without God, broken, incomplete, in need of love, mercy and grace.

When we worship, we exchange our perspective for God's. We stop focusing on what is happening around us and start looking at the One who holds all things together. Worship allows us to ascend, to go up where God's glory is revealed, and to see things through His eyes.

There is power in worship. Never forget that. It releases God's presence in our lives, it strengthens our faith, and it gives us the courage to keep pressing on.

But worship alone is not enough. When paired with prayer, you find a deep, intimate connection with the Father. Prayer is where you lay down your burdens and pick up His strength. It is where the impossible becomes possible because you are no longer relying on your own abilities but on the power of God. God himself is our greatest reward. And when we have Him, we have everything.

Prayer is the oxygen for our souls, and just like we cannot live without breathing, we can't thrive without prayer. It is not a ritual or a religious obligation. It is a lifeline, a conversation with the God who loves us.

When you pray, you ascend higher. You start to see the world as God sees it. You begin to understand His will for your life, and your heart aligns with His heart and His will.

The Call to Revival

Revival is what God is calling us to today. But it starts with us. Revival begins in the hearts of those who are willing to go up, to surrender everything to God and live in His presence. It is birthed in prayer and sustained by worship. It is not merely emotional experiences or exciting services, but a deep, inward transformation that spills over into every area of life.

We often think revival is something that happens *to* us, but in reality, it's something God *does* through us. It happens when we draw near to Him, when we refuse to settle for anything less than His presence. It happens when we let go of the high places in our lives and allow God to occupy the throne of our hearts.

Revival is personal before it is corporate. It starts with a willingness to come up, to climb the mountain, and to seek God with everything we have. The question is, how high do you want to go? Are you willing to let go of the things that are holding you back? Are you ready to destroy the high places in your life and occupy the heavenly places God has reserved for you?

Stay Up Here

May you be as at home in God as He is in you! God is not looking for people who will just come to Him when they feel like it, He's looking for people who will dwell with Him. The truth is many want the blessings of God without the commitment to stay close to Him. But the secret to a life of power, joy, and peace is staying connected to the source—staying in His presence.

You must run on His oil and not yours. When you try in your own strength to live this life it will consume and destroy you, but when you live in the presence of God, you do not burn out. You do not grow weary because you are continually refreshed by the oil of His Spirit. The oil that keeps burning and never gets tired is only found in one place. In His presence on holy ground. There is no shortcut or 'fake it until you make it' way. Nothing but God Himself can sustain the Christian's fire! Without OIL we mirror the foolish virgins who cried: "My lamp has burnt out, I have no power left and I have no way to make it come alive again."

Be assured... There's great power that comes when you choose to stay up, when you decide that nothing in this world is worth losing your connection with God. The enemy will try to pull you down. The distractions of life will try to consume your attention. But when you stay in God's presence, you rise above the noise. You live from a place of peace, strength, and confidence, knowing that the God who called you up is the same God who will keep you up.

God is calling each of us to ascend higher, to live in a constant state of worship, prayer, and revival. It is time to go up, to leave behind the things that weigh us down, and to step into the fullness of His presence. The journey will not always be easy. There will be moments when the climb feels steep, and the distractions of life try to pull you back down. But remember this: God is with you. He is cheering you on, inviting you to come closer, to see things from His perspective, and to experience the fullness of life in His presence.

The invitation is open. Will you accept it? Will you go up?

Part One - Intimacy And Worship

Imagine God's voice calling, *"Come closer, come closer."* Can you hear Him? He is inviting you to step up! He wants you to go beyond where you are, or even where you have been, into heavenly places with Him. He wants to reveal Himself to you, to show you His heart and His love in ways that will transform you. But to see it, you have to answer His call and come to Him.

Sound too simple? Well, it's true. All you have to do is show up, and God will take care of the rest. He will equip you, prepare you, and guide you precisely where you need to go.

Living a life of intimacy with God is not about doing more or being better. It is about a heart that longs to be near Him. James 4:8 says, *"Draw near to God and He will draw near to you."* God desires closeness with you even more than you could ever imagine or comprehend. When you take that first step toward Him, He meets you right there.

Too many of us believe that God is distant, hard to reach, or reluctant to meet with us. But that is not the truth. Just as He called Moses to the mountain, He is calling you to come up here. With every step closer, He reveals more of Himself. God is not far off—He is waiting, eager for you to draw near.

There is nothing in this world that can replace God's presence. You can search for fulfillment in countless ways, but only God's presence will satisfy your deepest needs. *"In Your presence is fullness of joy,"* declares Psalm 16:11. When you choose to live in His presence, your whole world changes. It is not that life becomes easy, but your perspective shifts. You see that the One who is with you is far more than anything that you face or can come against you. Worship becomes more than just a song; it becomes your life's response to His love. You stop striving for approval and start resting in His grace.

Intimacy comes through worship. Worship is not confined to music, a hymn or a Sunday service. Sadly, that is what so many have been led to believe, but that's not it. Worship is a lifestyle, a choice to lift your eyes above and focus on the One who created you. Worship is how you love, how you serve, how you live. When you encounter God's presence, worship overflows. It is giving your whole self—your thoughts, your words, your actions—as an offering to Him. In worship, we remember that He deserves everything we have to give. And as we lift Him up, He lifts us higher. You cannot lift Him up and not be drawn higher yourself.

Jesus continuously calls us to go higher.

He would go up a mountain, and His disciples would follow, eager to be close, willing to climb. It is no different for us. Worship is not meant to be something we turn to only on Sundays. It is about choosing every day to leave behind the distractions and step into His presence. It is about setting our hearts and minds on things above, where true life is found.

God's call is always to come closer, always to rise higher. He does not want you to just visit His presence; He wants you to live there. No matter where you are in your journey, His invitation stands—He is calling you to rise, to come up and experience Him more deeply than ever before.

Are you ready? The invitation is open. *"Come to me!"*

It is time to step into His presence and discover a life richer, deeper, and more fulfilling than anything this world could offer.

1

The Call To Come Closer

The more we respond to God's call, the more we discover that there is always more of God to experience.

The beauty of this invitation lies in the fact that God already knows us fully, yet He desires for us to know Him more deeply.

God, who is infinite, invites us to explore His endless nature. Isn't that amazing? There is no end to the depths of His love, His wisdom, and His presence. Every time we come closer, He reveals more, yet leaves us longing for even deeper connection.

This journey is about *knowing* God, but it is also about being *transformed* in the process. The closer we get to Him, the more we reflect His heart.

What is even more incredible is that this invitation is for everyone, no matter where you are in life. Whether you are just starting your faith journey, or you've been walking with God for decades, there is always a fresh invitation to go higher. God does not reserve intimacy for the "spiritual elite." He offers it to all who are willing to come. It is never too late to respond to His call, and it's never too early to begin. Every step we take toward Him is a step into a deeper, more fulfilling life.

When God calls us closer, it is not just to make us feel better or offer comfort, though those things often come with His presence. It is because He wants us to see the world from His perspective. Our everyday lives are filled with distractions, worries, and things that can cloud our vision. But God is calling us to lift our eyes higher, to rise above the noise, and experience His presence in a way that transforms everything.

Draw Near and See Differently

In the everyday hustle of life, it is easy to focus on what's directly in front of us. We get caught up in the tangible—the things we can see, touch, and manage on our own. But God is continually inviting us to go beyond that. He is calling us to come closer and see things from a different perspective, *His* perspective.

God's perspective is always higher than ours, and the closer we come to Him, the more clearly we see. Things that once seemed like insurmountable problems suddenly look small when we view them from His vantage point. The mountains we face in our daily lives are dwarfed by the greatness of His power and love. It is not that our problems disappear, but they lose their grip on our hearts as we focus on the One who is greater than anything we face.

Drawing near to God also allows us to see ourselves differently. We begin to understand that our identity is found in Him, not in our accomplishments, failures, or the opinions of others. In His presence, we see who we truly are—His beloved children, chosen, loved, and accepted. This shift in perspective changes everything. We are no longer striving to prove ourselves or earn approval. Instead, we rest in the knowledge that we are already accepted by the One whose opinion matters most.

When we draw near to God, we step into His presence, and in that place, everything changes. The challenges that seemed insurmountable from our human vantage point suddenly shrink when we see them through His eyes. The decisions we could not make become clearer when we trust His wisdom. As we rise to His level, we begin to realise that He is not just calling us to comfort us but to transform the way we live and think.

Elisha and His Servant

Elisha and his servant lived during a time of war between Israel and the king of Aram. The king of Aram was frustrated because every time he planned an attack on Israel, Elisha, the prophet of God, would warn the king of Israel, allowing him to evade capture. When the king of Aram discovered that Elisha was the one revealing his plans, he sent a large army to capture him, surrounding the city of Dothan, where Elisha was staying.

Elisha's servant woke up early in the morning, went outside, and saw the enemy army, horses, chariots, and soldiers, completely encircling the city. Terrified, he ran back to Elisha and cried, *"Oh no, my lord! What shall we do?"* (2 Kings 6:15). The situation seemed hopeless, and the servant could only see the immediate danger right in front of him.

But Elisha, in calm confidence, responded, *"Don't be afraid. Those who are with us are more than those who are with them"* (2 Kings 6:16). This must have sounded strange to the servant. All he could see was the enemy army. But Elisha could see something the servant could not. Because he was living close to God, he saw with spiritual eyes, not just natural ones.

Then, Elisha prayed, *"Open his eyes, Lord, so that he may see."* And as the Lord opened the servant's eyes, he saw the hills full of horses and chariots of fire surrounding Elisha (2 Kings 6:17). In that moment, the servant's perspective was completely changed. What had seemed like a hopeless situation was actually under God's control the entire time.

When we draw near to God, He often reveals the "bigger picture" to us, just as He did for Elisha's servant. Without God's perspective, the servant could only see his immediate circumstances. But when God opened his eyes, he saw that God's protection was far greater than the threat they faced.

This story reminds us that God's reality is often very different from what we perceive or expect. Drawing near to Him in times of fear and confusion helps us to look beyond our immediate challenges and see the greater reality of His presence and power. It is a reminder that we are never alone, and that God's resources far outweigh any obstacle we face.

When we seek God, He opens our eyes to see that His plans are bigger, His resources are limitless, and His protection surrounds us. Our perspective widens as we begin to understand that He is always in control, even when we feel overwhelmed.

Joy and Peace

Current opinion is that true joy and peace is not possible in this world, but when a person truly lives continually in God's presence, His presence makes it normal to dwell in a place of unshakable joy and peace. There is no substitute for it. The world offers many distractions, things that promise temporary satisfaction or relief, but only God's presence can fill the deep longing in our hearts. In His presence, we find a peace that surpasses all understanding and a joy that cannot be matched by anything else. It is like a spring of living water that wants to keep springing up irrespective of any attempts to stop it.

The fullness of joy that comes from living in God's presence is something the world can never offer. It is a joy that remains steady even in the midst of trials and hardship because it's not based on external circumstances. When we live in His presence, our hearts are anchored in His love, and we are able to face life's challenges with a peace that transcends our understanding. This joy is not fleeting, but a constant source of strength for our souls.

Living in His presence also brings a deep sense of purpose. When we dwell in the presence of God, we begin to see our lives through the lens of His greater plan. We start to understand that we are part of something much bigger than ourselves. Our daily tasks, interactions, and decisions take on new meaning as we realize that we are co-laborers with Christ in bringing His Kingdom to earth. His presence empowers us to live lives that are marked by purpose and passion.

When we make the decision to live in God's presence, it transforms our daily lives. It is no longer about going through the motions or just getting by. Living in His presence means waking up each day with an awareness of His nearness, with a heart that is constantly turned toward Him and a purpose that means something. It means trusting that no matter what challenges we face that day, He is with us, guiding us, and giving us the strength to keep moving forward.

Mary and Martha

Be still (har·pū -stop what you're doing) *and know that I am God!* (Psalm 46:10) Let's reflect on the story of Mary and Martha for a moment. As Jesus travelled through a village, He entered the home of two sisters, Mary and Martha. Martha welcomed Him into their home and immediately busied herself with preparations. She was focused on making sure everything was perfect, running back and forth to serve her guest. But Mary, on the other hand, chose to sit at Jesus' feet, listening intently to His words.

While Martha was working hard, she became frustrated with Mary's lack of help. She approached Jesus and said, *"Lord, don't you care that my sister has left me to do the work by myself? Tell her to help me!"* (Luke 10:40). Martha was consumed by the tasks in front of her, missing out on the joy of simply being in Jesus' presence.

Martha loved Jesus, but everyday while her worshipper's hearts yearned to sit at Jesus feet, like an invisible force, her world kept pulling her into its responsibilities, tasks, functions and concerns. This is real for so many. We forget this world has gravity. Gravity in the natural is the earth's ability to draw everything to its centre. The only way to loosen its grip is to apply a stronger commitment in the opposite direction. Because of this kind of gravity going down into the world is easy, but climbing the mountain of worship and prayer will take choosing the better thing.

Jesus responded to Martha with words that gently redirected her focus: *"Martha, Martha,"* He said, *"you are worried and upset about many things, but few things are needed—or indeed only one. Mary has chosen what is better, and it will not be taken away from her"* (Luke 10:41-42).

Martha's intentions were good. She wanted to serve and honour Jesus by taking care of the practical details. This was not a bad or wrong thing. Jesus even commended her heart in serving. But in her busyness, she missed the opportunity to experience the joy that Mary found. Mary experienced the joy that comes from being close to God. She chose to sit at Jesus' feet, taking in every word, letting her heart rest in His presence. She was not distracted by what needed to be done or what others expected of her. Instead, she was fully present, filled with a joy that only comes from intimacy with the Lord.

Mary's example shows us that the joy of being close to God is not about productivity or accomplishment; it's about presence. She delighted in simply being with Jesus, allowing His words to fill her with peace and contentment. Does this mean Mary had no part in serving? No. She just understood serving should flow out of presence not out of obligation.

This story reminds us that while the demands of life can often pull us in many directions, there is a deeper joy that comes from choosing to be with God, even when there is much to be done. The joy we find in His presence is a joy that fills our souls, renews our spirits, and brings true rest to our hearts. When we prioritize closeness with God, we tap into a joy that transcends circumstances and endures through every season of life.

Just as Jesus told Martha, we, too, are invited to choose what is better, to choose the joy that is found at His feet. When we draw near to God, we find a joy that nothing else in this world can offer, a joy that truly satisfies.

Ascending Higher

Whenever God calls us to come closer, it is an invitation to rise above the ordinary and step into the extraordinary.

In the Old Testament, we see many examples of God calling people to higher places. Moses went up the mountain to receive the commandments. Elijah ascended Mount Carmel to pray for rain. Each time, God revealed something extraordinary to those who were willing to go up. The higher we go with God, the more we see and experience of His power, His love, and His will for our lives. He calls us higher, not just for our own benefit, but so that we can bring His Kingdom to earth in new ways.

Ascending higher in God often means leaving behind the familiar. It means stepping out of our comfort zones and trusting Him to lead us into the unknown. This can be scary at times, but it is in those moments of stepping out in faith that we experience the greatest growth. The view from the top is always worth the climb, and the higher we go, the more we are transformed by His presence.

Consider Moses, who was called up to the mountain to meet with God. He had to leave the distractions of the people, the noise of everyday life, and step into a holy place where God could speak to him. When Moses ascended, he not only saw God's glory but received His commands, His direction, and a renewed sense of purpose. It was in that place that God answered all Moses' questions, reassured him of His faithfulness and revealed His capacity to help Moses with every one of his insecurities.

This is true for us too. As we ascend, there are things we must deal with. In the Old Testament, high places were often associated with idolatry. They were places where people worshipped false gods, and they became stumbling blocks for the Israelites.

Today, we might not have physical high places in the same way, but there are still areas in our lives where we allow things other than God to take priority. These are the high places that can hinder our relationship with Him.

High places are often subtle, and they do not always appear as blatant idols. They can be things we rely on for security, comfort, or identity that replace our trust in God. Sometimes, our careers, relationships, or even our own desires can become high places if we elevate them above God. These high places may provide temporary satisfaction, but they cannot offer the lasting fulfilment that comes from living fully surrendered to Him.

Tearing down these high places requires honesty and humility. We must be willing to ask God to search our hearts and reveal anything that has taken His rightful place in our lives. This can be a painful process, as it often requires us to let go of things we have held onto for security or comfort. But as we surrender these high places, we make room for God's presence to fill every area of our lives. It is in this place of surrender that true freedom and intimacy with God are found.

High places can be anything we lift above God—our ambitions, our fears, our relationships, even our own desires. These things become idols when they take precedence over our pursuit of God. And just as the Israelites had to destroy the high places in their land, we must be willing to tear down the high places in our hearts.

The Cost of Closeness

There is a cost to intimacy with God. The cost of intimacy is the forsaking of all others for the prize of the ONE! Drawing closer to Him means letting go of the things that hold us back. It means surrendering our own desires, our own plans, and even our own comforts.

But do you know what? *The cost is worth it.*

Closeness with God demands our attention, time, and focus. It requires us to prioritize His presence over our own plans, to make room for Him in our busy schedules. This might mean sacrificing some comforts or letting go of certain distractions, but the reward is a deeper, more fulfilling relationship with Him. The closer we come to God, the more we realize that nothing in this world compares to the joy of knowing Him.

The cost of intimacy also involves vulnerability. To come closer to God, we must be willing to be transparent with Him, to allow Him to see the deepest parts of our hearts. This can be uncomfortable, but it is in those moments of vulnerability that we experience the healing and transformation that only His presence can bring. As we surrender our hearts to Him, He meets us with grace, mercy, and love.

Jesus said, *"Whoever wants to be my disciple must deny themselves and take up their cross daily and follow me"* (Luke 9:23). The call to come closer is also a call to die to ourselves. It is a call to lay down our lives, our agendas, and our desires, and take up the cross of Christ.

I know that sounds like a lot, but the reward is much bigger than anything we sacrifice. In doing so, we find *true life*.

Responding to the Call

The call to come closer is not one that can be or should be ignored. It is not something we can put off for another time or wait until we feel more ready. God is calling us now, today, to draw near to Him, to ascend to new heights of intimacy and relationship.

This is a call that requires action. We cannot passively wait for intimacy with God to happen. We must be intentional about seeking Him, carving out time to be in His presence, and pursuing His heart. The longer we wait to respond, the more opportunities we miss to experience the fullness of life He offers.

The time to draw near is **NOW**, and the choice is ours to make.

Responding to this call means saying yes to God in every area of our lives. It means surrendering our plans, our dreams, and our fears, and trusting that His way is better than ours. It is an ongoing decision to keep coming closer, even when it feels uncomfortable or difficult. But with each step we take toward Him, we find that He is already there, waiting for us with open arms.

He stands at the door and knocks, waiting for us to respond. But He will not force His way in. The choice is ours. Will we open the door and invite Him into every part of our lives? Will we respond to His call to come closer, or will we stay where we are, content with a distant relationship?

The Journey Upward

The journey upward is not always easy, but it is *always* worth it.

As we respond to God's call to come closer, we will encounter Him in ways we never have before. We will experience His presence in ways that transform us from the inside out. And as we ascend, we will see more clearly, love more deeply, and live more fully.

Each step upward brings new challenges, but it also brings new revelations of God's love and character. The journey may require perseverance, but the rewards are eternal. The closer we come to God, the more we reflect His heart and His glory to the world around us. Our lives become a testimony of His goodness and grace, and others are drawn to Him because of the transformation they see in us.

As we ascend, we also find that we are not climbing alone. God is with us every step of the way, guiding, strengthening, and encouraging us. His Spirit empowers us to keep moving forward, even when the climb feels steep. And when we reach new heights, we discover that the view is more beautiful than we ever imagined. The journey is worth it because the destination is God Himself.

The invitation has been given, and the door is open. All you must do is step in.

2

Living In His Presence

Psalm 16:11 (NKJV) - "In Your presence is fullness of joy."

The heartbeat of the Christian life is more than simply knowing about God, it is living in His presence.

Psalm 16:11 reminds us of this truth: *"In Your presence is fullness of joy; at Your right hand are pleasures forevermore."* The fullness of life, joy, and peace can only be found in the presence of God. Living in God's presence is not meant to be an occasional moment but a continual, abiding reality. As Jesus said in John 15:4 (NKJV), *"Abide in Me, and I in you."* When the Lord is your Shepherd... then you will want for nothing! In Him is more than you will ever need or want.

Abiding in Christ means remaining in His presence, allowing His Spirit to fill every area of our lives. This chapter is about moving from occasional encounters with God to dwelling in His presence continually. It is an invitation to a deeper life, one where God's presence becomes the air we breathe. Not just in general, but moment by moment every breath is only possible because He gives it. When we understand the magnitude of what it means to live in His presence, everything else in our lives shifts into its proper place. The things that once consumed our time and attention fade in comparison to the glory of His presence.

God never intended for us to be distant from Him. His original design, seen in the Garden of Eden, was one of intimacy and constant fellowship. Adam and Eve walked with God daily, experiencing the fullness of His presence. Though sin disrupted that closeness, God, through Christ, made a way for us to return to that kind of intimacy. Now, through the work of Jesus, He invites us once again to live in His presence—to walk with Him every day, not just on occasion. This is the kind of life that transforms, renews, and empowers us to live out our calling with joy and purpose.

Ever wonder why this world wants to interrupt, crowd out or redefine this living in God's presence? Because that is exactly what lured Adam and Eve from their life lived in His presence. They walked, talked and lived personally with God until they moved away looking for something else. As it was then, so it is now, nothing can fill the space in our lives that was designed for God's presence. There are no substitutes for it. We may seek fulfillment in relationships, careers, adventures, or personal achievements, but they all pale in comparison to the joy that comes from living in God's presence. The pursuits of the world promise satisfaction, but they often leave us more drained, more empty, and more in need than when we began. The promises of the devil and this world are pure lies. Only God's presence offers lasting fulfillment, and once we taste it, there can be no turning back, nothing else will compare or even come close.

When we try to fill our hearts with temporary pleasures, we quickly realize their inadequacy. The job promotion, the relationship, the achievement—all these things can offer temporary happiness, but they can never replace the deep, soul-satisfying joy that comes from being in the presence of our Creator. The joy of God's presence is a different kind of joy—it is deeper, more enduring, and more constant than anything the world can provide. It is a joy that sustains us through life's toughest challenges and gives us peace that defies understanding.

Without God's presence, we are left to our own devices, trying to navigate life's complexities on our own. But in His presence, we find fullness of joy, clarity, wisdom, and strength. Living in God's presence is what enables us to live victoriously, regardless of our circumstances. It is the key to spiritual growth, emotional health, and personal peace. When we live in His presence, we tap into His power, and everything in our lives aligns with His will and purpose.

The world offers countless distractions—mirages that promise satisfaction but leave us empty. These distractions are like chasing after the wind, always elusive, never delivering what they promise. But God's presence is different. It does not change, and it doesn't fade away. It is eternal and unwavering. When we choose to live in His presence, we find everything we need for life, joy, and peace. This is why it is so critical to learn how to live in His presence continually, rather than relying on fleeting moments of connection.

There is a clear difference between simply visiting God's presence and living in it. Many Christians treat God's presence like a place they visit on Sundays or during moments of crisis. They come in and out, seeking a temporary fix or a brief comfort. But God never intended for us to live like that. His desire is for us to remain in His presence, to live there continually, where His love and power flow through us every day.

Living in God's presence means that His Spirit saturates every moment, not just the "holy" moments. It means being aware of His nearness whether we are in a worship service, at work, or spending time with family. It is about walking with Him, listening for His voice, and responding to His lead. As we make His presence our dwelling place, we begin to experience life as He intended it—filled with peace, joy, and purpose.

The Prodigal Son

The parable of the Prodigal Son explains how nothing can fill our hearts except for God. Jesus tells the story of a father who has two sons. The younger son, eager to experience life on his own terms, asked his father for his share of the inheritance. His father granted his request, and with his newfound wealth, the younger son left home and traveled to a distant country. There, he indulged in a life of excess, spending his money on wild living and chasing after things that promised happiness and satisfaction.

But as quickly as his wealth came, it was gone. A severe famine struck the land, and with no money left, the son found himself in desperate need. He ended up taking a job feeding pigs, a task that would have been disgraceful for a Jewish man. He was so hungry that even the food he fed to the pigs began to look appetizing. In this moment of complete emptiness, he realized that all the things he had pursued had left him with nothing but hunger and regret.

Then he had a moment of clarity. He thought to himself, *"How many of my father's hired servants have food to spare, and here I am starving to death! I will set out and go back to my father and say to him: 'Father, I have sinned against heaven and against you. I am no longer worthy to be called your son; make me like one of your hired servants.'"* (Luke 15:17-19).

The younger son finally recognized that everything he had been chasing could not fill the emptiness inside him. The pleasures, the freedom, the wealth—all of it left him broken and alone. And so, he decided to return to his father, humbly acknowledging his mistakes.

As he approached home, his father saw him from a distance and was filled with compassion. The father ran to his son, embraced him, and kissed him. The son began to apologize, but his father interrupted him, calling for his servants to bring the best robe, a ring, and sandals for his feet. He then ordered a feast, saying, *"For this son of mine was dead and is alive again; he was lost and is found."* (Luke 15:24).

This story reflects our tendency to seek fulfillment in things other than God. Like the prodigal son, we may pursue wealth, pleasure, status, or independence, believing these things will make us happy. But, just as he discovered, these pursuits often leave us feeling emptier and more lost than before. The things of this world cannot satisfy our deepest needs—they can't fill the void in our hearts that only God's love can occupy.

The Prodigal Son's story shows us that no matter how far we wander or how deeply we have tried to fill our lives with things other than God, He is always waiting, ready to welcome us back with open arms. The father's response in the story is a powerful picture of God's love for us. When we realize the emptiness of worldly pursuits and turn back to Him, we find that He is not only willing but eager to restore us, to embrace us, and to fill our lives with a joy and peace that nothing else can provide.

This story serves as a reminder that we can find true satisfaction and fulfillment only in God. The things of this world may offer temporary pleasure, but they can never fill the deep, eternal longing within us. When we return to God, we find the love, acceptance, and purpose we were created for, a life lived in relationship with our Father, who delights in our return and rejoices over us with open arms.

Abiding in Christ

In John 15:4 (NKJV), Jesus commands us to abide in Him: *"Abide in Me, and I in you. As the branch cannot bear fruit by itself unless it abides in the vine, neither can you, unless you abide in Me."* The imagery here is powerful—just as a branch cannot survive apart from the vine, we cannot live the life God has called us to live apart from His presence. Abiding in Christ is the foundation of everything we do as believers. It is not simply an instruction; it is a lifeline.

Abiding is remaining connected to Him. It is a posture of dependence, where we rely on His strength rather than our own. It is about continual communion with Him, where His presence influences our thoughts, actions, and attitudes. Just as a branch draws its nourishment and life from the vine, we must draw our life and strength from Jesus. Without Him, we can do nothing of eternal significance.

This call to abide is not a passive one—it requires intentionality. It requires us to make space in our lives for God, to prioritize our relationship with Him above all else. In a world that constantly pulls at our attention, abiding means choosing to remain in God's presence, even when distractions try to lure us away. It means making time for prayer, worship, and reading His Word, allowing His Spirit to fill us and guide us in all that we do.

Too many Christians today attempt to live a "plug-in, plug-out" Christianity. They plug into God's presence when they need something, then unplug when they feel they can handle life on their own. But Jesus does not call us to a life of occasional connection; He called us to abide. Abiding is a continual connection. A branch does not disconnect from the vine and reconnect when it feels like it—it remains grafted in at all times.

Abiding in Christ is not about striving or performing; it is about resting in who He is and what He has done for us. It is about knowing that our identity is found in Him, not in our accomplishments or failures. As we abide in Him, we are transformed from the inside out. His presence shapes us, molds us, and empowers us to live a life that brings glory to God.

To abide means to stay connected. It means to let God's Word dwell in us, to let His Spirit guide our every step. The more we abide in Him, the more we become like Him. His presence shapes us, molds us, and gives us the strength to live the life He has called us to.

The Transforming Power of His Presence

Living in God's presence transforms us. It changes our perspective, our priorities, and our hearts. When we are consistently in His presence, the things of this world lose their grip on us. The distractions, fears, and temptations that once seemed so important begin to fade away in the light of His glory. The more we dwell in His presence, the more we are transformed into His image.

God's presence has the power to heal, restore, and renew us. It is in His presence that we find healing for our wounds, strength for our weaknesses, and hope for our future. When we live in His presence, we are no longer defined by our past mistakes or our present struggles. We are defined by who God says we are—His beloved children, called and chosen for a purpose. His presence empowers us to live in freedom, joy, and boldness.

As we spend time in His presence, we begin to reflect His character more and more. Our thoughts become aligned with His thoughts, our desires with His desires. We begin to see the world through His eyes, and our hearts are filled with compassion, love, and mercy. This transformation is not something we can achieve on our own, but rather it is the work of the Holy Spirit within us as we remain in God's presence.

Peter's transformation is one of the most remarkable stories in the Bible. Imagine the despair he must have felt after denying Jesus, not once, but three times—each denial more painful than the last. The guilt and shame must have weighed heavily on him, clouding his heart and mind. This was the defining failure of a man who had sworn to stand by Jesus until the end.

Yet, when Peter encountered the risen Christ, something powerful happened. Jesus did not chastise him or hold his failures against him. Instead, He looked at Peter with love, offering him grace beyond understanding.

In that moment, Peter's heart was forever changed. Jesus took a man broken by shame and rebuilt him into someone filled with unshakable courage. No longer was Peter the fisherman plagued by fear or the man who crumbled under pressure. With each word Jesus spoke, Peter's past was redefined, his failures transformed into strength. And from then on, Peter walked a different path. He became a bold preacher, standing before crowds and proclaiming the truth with conviction, even when it meant facing persecution, prison, and ultimately, a martyr's death.

Peter's encounter with Jesus redefined his purpose, filling him with a passion to live—and if necessary, die—for the gospel. He went from being the man who ran in fear to the man who stood fearlessly, his life a testament to the power of God's forgiveness and the depth of Christ's love.

This is the kind of transformation that happens when we live in God's presence. We are no longer defined by our past mistakes or our failures. We are defined by who God says we are—His beloved children, called and chosen for a purpose. His presence empowers us to live in freedom, joy, and boldness. His presence makes us more like Him, giving us the strength and courage to walk in the fullness of our calling.

When we spend time in God's presence, the things that once held us back—fear, insecurity, and doubt—are replaced with faith, hope, and confidence. We are no longer bound by the limitations of this world because we are connected to the limitless power of God. His presence gives us the ability to overcome any obstacle and walk in victory, no matter what challenges we face.

Joy in His Presence

One of the greatest blessings of living in God's presence is the joy it brings. This joy is so much better than just being happy. It is full and overflowing. It bubbles up out of the eternal spring of life and revives every dry and thirsty place. As Psalm 16:11 says, *"In Your presence is fullness of joy."* This joy is not dependent on our circumstances or external conditions—it flows from the very heart of God. It is a joy that transcends the trials and difficulties of life, a joy that sustains us even in the darkest of times. In God's presence, we experience a joy that the world cannot offer.

This joy is not fleeting or temporary, but it is deep and abiding. It comes from knowing that we are loved by God, that we are secure in His hands, and that nothing can separate us from His love. When we live in His presence, our hearts are filled with peace and contentment, knowing that we belong to Him. The joy of God's presence is not an emotion that comes and goes—it is a state of being that flows from our relationship with Him.

When we live in His presence, we begin to see life differently. Our perspective shifts from focusing on what we do not have to what we do have in Him. We become more aware of His blessings, His provision, and His faithfulness. This awareness fills our hearts with gratitude, and that gratitude leads to joy. The more we focus on God's goodness, the more joy we experience, regardless of our circumstances.

This joy is a fruit of the Spirit, produced in us as we live in His presence.

When we live in His presence, our hearts are filled with gratitude and praise. This joy is contagious—it overflows from our lives and touches those around us. People are drawn to the joy that comes from living in God's presence because it is something the world cannot offer.

The joy of living in God's presence is not dependent on our external circumstances. It remains constant even when life is difficult because it is rooted in our relationship with God. His joy sustains us through trials, comforts us in sorrow, and gives us strength in times of weakness. This is the joy that Jesus promised when He said, *"These things I have spoken to you, that My joy may remain in you, and that your joy may be full"* (John 15:11, NKJV).

3

Worship As A Lifestyle

Romans 12:1 - "Offer your bodies as a living sacrifice, holy and pleasing to God—this is your true and proper worship."

Worship is far more than a song we sing on Sunday mornings. It is more than lifting our hands in a moment of praise. True worship is about laying our entire lives down before God as a living sacrifice, just as Romans 12:1 reminds us. When we offer ourselves—our desires, our plans, and our very beings—as a sacrifice, that becomes our genuine worship.

Worship, then, is not something we only do in church, it is the way we live every single day.

True worship requires the surrender of every part of us. It is not just about dedicating our time, but about giving God everything we are and everything we have. God is looking for worshipers who are willing to lay down their pride, their ambitions, and even their comforts in order to honor Him. This surrender is a lifestyle. Each day presents us with opportunities to surrender again, to offer ourselves on the altar of obedience and trust.

Worship is also a response. When we truly understand what God has done for us, worship naturally flows out of our hearts. His sacrifice calls for a response of devotion, surrender, and love. When we grasp the enormity of His grace, we no longer see worship as something to be performed, but a reflection of our gratitude and reverence. Worship becomes a natural expression of who we are in Him, and our lives reflect His glory in every aspect.

God is not just looking for people who know how to sing. How sad it would have been if only those with great voices and musical abilities were able to worship and enter the presence of God. No, it is far more than that. Our Father is looking for people who will surrender every part of their lives to Him. Worship is a response to God's love. When we truly grasp what God has done for us—how He laid down His own life through Jesus Christ—it compels us to offer everything we are back to Him. It is not just about what we give during a worship service but how we live the rest of our lives in response to His grace and mercy. Every decision, every conversation, and every action becomes an act of worship when it is done with a heart surrendered to God.

The greatest act of worship we can offer is our obedience. It is saying "yes" to God when He asks us to step out in faith, even when it is uncomfortable, inconvenient and expensive. It is loving others when it's difficult, forgiving when it's hard, and serving when it costs us something. That is what a life laid down in worship looks like. It is a life that points back to God, in everything we do. Our willingness to obey God, even in the small details, is a powerful form of worship that echoes beyond words and music.

Worship that comes from a surrendered heart is authentic worship. It is not about grand gestures or public displays; it is about a quiet, daily decision to place God at the center of everything we do. True worshipers live with an awareness that every moment is an opportunity to honor God. Whether in private moments of prayer or in interactions with others, their lives point to the greatness of God, reflecting His love and His will in every action.

Living Sacrifices: A Daily Offering

Romans 12:1 uses a powerful phrase: *"Offer your bodies as a living sacrifice."* This paints a picture of ongoing, daily worship. In the Old Testament, sacrifices were offered at the temple, and once they were burned on the altar, they were consumed. But here, we are called to be "living sacrifices," continually offering ourselves to God. This means that our worship does not stop at the altar; it continues in every aspect of our lives.

Being a living sacrifice requires daily surrender. It is a lifelong journey! Every day brings new challenges, new opportunities to surrender our will, and new moments where we must choose between our own desires and God's. This daily act of offering ourselves to God is what transforms us into His likeness. It is the process of refining, of becoming more like Christ, as we lay down our lives in obedience to Him.

The call to be a living sacrifice is also a call to live in humility. It means acknowledging that we cannot live this life on our own, that we need God's strength and grace to walk in holiness. Living as a sacrifice means giving up our rights, our preferences, and our comforts for the sake of others and for the glory of God. It is a life of self-denial that leads to deeper joy and fulfillment in Christ.

Our lives, when surrendered to God, become a constant offering. It is a daily choice to lay down our own desires, ambitions, and comforts in exchange for His will and His presence. Every morning when we wake up, we have the opportunity to offer our lives to God once again. It is in the mundane, everyday moments that true worship is cultivated. Whether you are at work, driving, or spending time with family, God calls us to offer those moments to Him. It is a life that says, "Lord, I'm here. Use me according to Your will."

Being a living sacrifice also means that we remain open and willing to let God change and mold us. Just as a sacrifice on the altar is consumed, we too are consumed by the refining fire of God's presence. His Spirit works in us, purifying our hearts and aligning our desires with His. This process can be uncomfortable, but it leads to transformation.

As we yield to God's will, He shapes us into vessels fit for His use, vessels that carry His presence and reflect His glory.

Living as a sacrifice can be uncomfortable. It requires letting go of control, trusting God's plan over our own. But there is a profound freedom that comes with surrender. When we truly surrender, we are no longer burdened by the need to have all the answers or make everything work out. We leave it in God's hands, trusting that His ways are higher than ours. In that place of surrender, we discover that worship is not a burden; it is a privilege.

The beautiful paradox of being a living sacrifice is that when we lay our lives down, we find real life in return. Jesus Himself said, *"Whoever loses their life for My sake will find it"* (Matthew 16:25, NKJV). This is the heart of worship. It is not just a song or an event; it is a life continually laid down in service and obedience to God. The more we surrender to Him, the more we experience the fullness of life that only He can provide. In losing our lives, we truly find them in Christ.

Abraham and Isaac: A Test of Faith

Worship adds fire to faith and faith brings passion to worship! Abraham had waited many years for the fulfillment of God's promise to give him a son. Finally, in his old age, he and his wife, Sarah, welcomed Isaac, the child through whom God promised to establish a great nation. Isaac represented not only Abraham's beloved son but also the fulfillment of God's covenant with him.

Then, seemingly out of nowhere, God gave Abraham an unfathomable command: *"Take your son, your only son, whom you love—Isaac—and go to the region of Moriah. Sacrifice him there as a burnt offering on a mountain I will show you."* (Genesis 22:2). This command must have shaken Abraham to his core. Isaac was not just his son—he was the very symbol of God's promise. Yet, Abraham's obedience was immediate. He did not delay or question; he simply set out with Isaac early the next morning.

As they traveled, Isaac noticed they had fire and wood but no lamb for the sacrifice. He asked his father, *"The fire and wood are here, but where is the lamb for the burnt offering?"* (Genesis 22:7). Abraham replied, *"God himself will provide the lamb for the burnt offering, my son."* His answer reflects a deep trust in God, even in the face of unimaginable sacrifice.

When they reached the place God had specified, Abraham built an altar, arranged the wood, and bound his son Isaac, laying him on the altar. Then, just as he reached out his hand to take the knife, the angel of the Lord called out to him from heaven, *"Abraham! Abraham! Do not lay a hand on the boy. Do not do anything to him. Now I know that you fear God, because you have not withheld from me your son, your only son."* (Genesis 22:11-12).

At that moment, Abraham looked up and saw a ram caught in a thicket. He took the ram and sacrificed it as a burnt offering in place of his son. This act was a foreshadowing of God's provision—the ultimate sacrifice that would one day come through Jesus, the Lamb of God.

Abraham's willingness to sacrifice Isaac is a powerful example of what it means to live a life fully surrendered to God. This was no small sacrifice; it was the very thing that represented Abraham's future, his legacy, and God's promise. Yet Abraham demonstrated that he valued obedience to God more than anything else, even the blessings he had received. He was willing to offer up everything back to God, trusting that God's purposes were higher than his own understanding.

Romans 12:1 echoes this kind of sacrifice: *"Therefore, I urge you, brothers and sisters, in view of God's mercy, to offer your bodies as a living sacrifice, holy and pleasing to God—this is your true and proper worship."* Living as a sacrifice means being willing to place our desires, our plans, and even our dearest treasures in God's hands, trusting Him with the outcomes. It means surrendering not just once, but continually, each day choosing to live a life that honors Him.

Abraham's story teaches us that living a life of sacrifice requires trust, obedience, and faith that God is good, even when we do not understand

His ways. In the end, God provided for Abraham, just as He always provides for us when we choose to trust Him with everything. And, ultimately, God has given us the perfect example of sacrifice through Jesus, who gave His life so that we might live.

This story calls us to examine our own lives and ask, *What am I holding back from God?*

Are we willing to live sacrificially, to place everything on the altar before Him, trusting that He knows best?

When we live in complete surrender, we find a deeper relationship with God, who always has greater plans for us than we can imagine.

Worship in Everything We Do

True worship is about more than the songs we sing or the moments we raise our hands in church. It is about the posture of our hearts in every aspect of life. Remember, worship is a lifestyle. When we grasp that worship is living for God in everything we do, we start to see our entire lives as an offering to Him. From the way we treat others to the way we conduct ourselves at work, every action can become an act of worship.

Worship should dictate every part of our lives when we invite God into every moment. It is the way we speak to our family, the way we serve our communities, and the way we respond to challenges. Our attitudes, actions, and thoughts reflect our devotion to God when we live with a worshipful heart. Worship as a lifestyle does not mean we ignore the practicalities of life, but that we approach those practicalities with a heart that seeks to honor God in all things.

When worship becomes a lifestyle, we begin to understand that God is present in the small, everyday moments just as much as He is in the significant, spiritual ones. We honor Him not just with our voices, but with our lives—how we spend our time, how we treat others, and how we manage the resources He has given us. In doing so, we live in a constant state of worship, reflecting God's goodness in all we do.

When we see life through the lens of worship, the mundane becomes sacred. Washing dishes, driving to work, and even our conversations with friends become opportunities to glorify God. Worship is about bringing God into every part of our day, acknowledging His presence and responding to His love. Every time we choose love over hate, forgiveness over bitterness, or humility over pride, we are worshipping God. It is in those small, everyday choices that we honor Him.

Jesus embodied this perfectly. His life was a continuous act of worship, a living testimony of His deep and unbroken connection with the Father. From His early days in the temple to His final hours on the cross, everything Jesus did was an offering of praise and devotion.

Consider the moment Jesus, at only twelve years old, stayed behind in the temple while His family journeyed home from Jerusalem. His parents, worried sick, found Him sitting among the teachers, listening and asking questions. When they asked why He had stayed behind, Jesus responded, *"Didn't you know I had to be in my Father's house?"* (Luke 2:49). Even at a young age, Jesus lived with an acute awareness of His purpose. This was not just an act of youthful curiosity, it was worship. Being in His Father's house, discussing the Scriptures, and seeking wisdom was how He honored God with His mind and heart.

Throughout His ministry, Jesus showed that worship meant reaching out to those who were often overlooked. When He healed the leper, it was worship. Lepers were cast out of society, shunned, and feared. By reaching out and touching the leper, Jesus demonstrated the Father's heart. He valued the ones whom society deemed unworthy and showed that worship involves loving others as God loves them. His actions glorified the Father by revealing God's boundless mercy and compassion, even to those on the fringes of society.

One of the most vivid examples of worship in Jesus' life is found in the story of Lazarus. When Lazarus died, Jesus traveled to Bethany, where Martha and Mary, Lazarus's sisters, were grieving. Even in His grief, Jesus took a moment to lift His eyes and say, *"Father, I thank you that you have heard me."* (John 11:41). His words reflect a deep sense of trust and reverence. Jesus knew what He was about to do, but He took a moment to acknowledge the Father, even in the midst of heartache. His prayer was not a plea but an affirmation of God's faithfulness. Raising Lazarus was also an act of worship, a testament to God's power over life and death.

When Jesus fed the five thousand, He again showed us worship in action. Surrounded by hungry people, Jesus took the loaves and the fishes, lifted His eyes to heaven, and gave thanks. He did not perform a grand ritual or wait for a perfect setting. Instead, in the middle of a crowd, He took what little they had, gave thanks, and God multiplied it (Matthew 14:19). By giving thanks before the miracle, Jesus showed that worship is rooted in gratitude and faith. It is the humble act of acknowledging that every blessing comes from the Father's hand.

Even in His moments of solitude, Jesus modeled worship as a lifestyle. The Gospels frequently mention how He would withdraw to quiet places to pray. One of the most powerful examples of this is in the Garden of Gethsemane. On the night of His arrest, Jesus knelt in the garden, His heart heavy with sorrow. Knowing what lay ahead, He still prayed, *"Father, if you are willing, take this cup from me; yet not my will, but yours be done."* (Luke 22:42). In His darkest hour, Jesus' prayer was one of surrender. This was not just obedience; it was worship. He chose to honor the Father's will over His own, even when it meant enduring the cross.

The cross itself is the ultimate act of worship. Jesus' life culminated in this moment, a sacrifice that would forever change humanity. As He hung there, beaten and bruised, He continued to glorify the Father. With one of His final breaths, He cried out, *"Father, into your hands I commit my spirit."* (Luke 23:46). Even in death, Jesus gave everything to the Father, offering His life as the highest act of worship. Jesus did not just live a life of worship, He showed us that true worship is a complete surrender of our will to God's, a daily decision to glorify Him in all things.

Following in His footsteps, reminds us that worship is about more than what happens in a church service. It is about how we live every moment in response to God's goodness.

When we live with this perspective, we begin to realize that worship is not something we turn on and off. It is a continual offering of our lives. We start to see that worship is not confined to music or specific moments of devotion. Instead, it is a constant flow of gratitude, service, and surrender that touches every area of our existence. Living in this way transforms not only how we relate to God but how we relate to others. Everything becomes an opportunity to reflect His love and His glory.

Surrender: The Heart of Worship

At the core of worship is surrender. Without surrender, worship becomes just a ritual or a performance. When we truly surrender to God—laying down our own desires, plans, and ambitions—that's when worship becomes real. Worship is about giving God what He deserves, not what is convenient for us. It is about laying down our entire lives in gratitude for what He has done.

Surrendering is not easy. It means letting go of control and trusting God's plan, even when we do not understand it. But that is where the beauty of worship lies. When we surrender, we are acknowledging that God is greater than we are. We are saying, "God, I trust You more than I trust myself. I give You everything." It is in that place of surrender that authentic worship is born.

Surrender requires vulnerability. We must open our hearts to God, allowing Him to work in areas we may have kept hidden or protected. It involves trusting that His plans are better than ours, even when it requires giving up something we cherish. As we let go of our control, God steps in to transform our lives in ways we could never imagine. Surrendering to God is not about losing ourselves, it is about discovering the fullness of who we were created to be in Him.

One of the greatest obstacles to true worship is our desire for control. We like to hold on to our plans, our comfort, and our security. But God calls us to lay those things down. Just as Abraham was willing to sacrifice Isaac, we are called to offer the things we hold dear to God, trusting that He knows what is best. True worship begins with an open hand, letting go of everything that competes with our devotion to God.

Surrender is a daily choice. Each day, we have the opportunity to surrender our lives afresh to God. As we do, we experience the joy and freedom that comes from living in alignment with His will. Worship becomes more than a song—it becomes the way we live our lives, fully surrendered to God. Every moment of our day can become an opportunity to surrender, trust, and honor Him.

As we cultivate this posture of surrender, our worship deepens. We begin to recognize that surrender is not about what we lose, but about what we gain. The peace that comes from laying down our lives in worship is profound. It frees us from the burden of trying to control everything and opens us to the fullness of God's plans. In this act of surrender, we become vessels for His purposes, ready and willing to be used by Him in whatever way He chooses.

Living with an Eternal Perspective

Worship is about keeping our eyes on eternity. When we live with an eternal perspective, everything changes. The things that once seemed so important—the pursuit of success, recognition, or material possessions—begin to fade in the light of God's glory. We realize that life is not about accumulating treasures here on earth, but about storing up treasures in heaven. True worship comes from a heart that is fixed on eternity, longing to glorify God in everything.

An eternal perspective shifts our focus away from temporary gains and onto the lasting impact of our relationship with God. When we fix our eyes on eternity, our priorities change. We start to see that what matters most is not the success we achieve or the accolades we receive but the legacy we leave for God's Kingdom. Worship becomes more than just a moment; it becomes an investment in eternity, a reflection of our desire to see God's purposes fulfilled on earth.

Living with an eternal perspective helps us navigate the trials and challenges of life with grace. Instead of being consumed by the pressures of this world, we can endure hardship with hope, knowing that our lives are part of something much greater. Worshiping God through our trials brings us into alignment with His eternal purposes. Our trials, though temporary, can be opportunities to glorify Him and point others toward His eternal promises.

When we live with an eternal perspective, our priorities shift. We start to see people differently. We start to view every relationship, every interaction as an opportunity to reflect the love of Christ. Worship becomes about more than just what happens in church; it becomes about how we treat others, how we spend our time, and how we use the resources God has given us. It is about living in a way that points others to Jesus.

Paul reminds us in Romans 12:2 not to conform to the patterns of this world but to be transformed by the renewing of our minds. This transformation happens when we live with an eternal perspective. When we fix our eyes on Jesus and the life He has called us to live, we are no longer swayed by the temporary pleasures of this world. Instead, we are motivated by a desire to worship God with our lives, knowing that every sacrifice we make for His kingdom has eternal significance.

Living with eternity in mind gives our worship depth and meaning. We begin to understand that our lives here on earth are just a small part of God's grand plan. As we worship Him in the here and now, we are participating in something that extends far beyond our own lives. This understanding fuels our worship and strengthens our resolve to live every day in a way that honors Him. It makes every sacrifice worth it because we know that we are part of something eternal.

Worship as a Response to God's Love

Worship is our echo to God's first love. The first motivation for worship was stated by God not us. Even when we choose to draw near, worship is not something initiated by us. It is a response to what God has already done. When we truly understand the magnitude of God's love for us, worship becomes the natural response. We worship because He first loved us. We offer our lives as a living sacrifice because He offered His life for us. Worship is the overflow of a heart that has been touched by grace.

God's love for us is not dependent on our performance or our efforts. It is a love that is constant, unchanging, and unconditional. This kind of love calls for a response, not out of obligation, but out of gratitude. When we experience God's love, our hearts are stirred to worship. Every act of service, every prayer, every song becomes a response to the overwhelming love that God has poured out on us through Christ.

Worship is not just about expressing our love for God; it is about experiencing His love for us. As we worship, we are reminded of His goodness, His mercy, and His faithfulness. Our worship is a reflection of how much we value Him, and it's an acknowledgment of His worthiness. The more we understand His love, the deeper our worship becomes. It moves beyond words and songs, transforming our lives into a continuous offering of gratitude and devotion.

When we consider the lengths to which God went to redeem us—sending His only Son to die in our place—it compels us to respond in worship. We do not worship out of obligation or duty; we worship because we are in awe of His love. Every act of worship, whether it is singing a song, serving others, or spending time in prayer, is an expression of our gratitude for what He has done.

Our worship is also a reflection of how much we value God. When we truly value something, we invest in it. If we value our relationship with God, our lives will reflect that. Worship becomes more than just something we do one day a week—it becomes a way of life. Every decision, every action, and every word is an opportunity to honor God and express our love for Him.

The most profound worship arises from a heart that has been captivated by God's love. It is love that compels us to lay down our lives as a living sacrifice. The more we experience His love, the more we are drawn into deeper worship. Our response is not about trying to earn His love, but about expressing the love He has already lavished upon us.

Worship is the overflow of a heart that has been transformed by grace!

When you live continuously in this state of worship your Sundays will always be supercharged, because it will be the overflow of what you are already living in!

Part Two - The Power Of Prayer

Prayer is the lifeline of every believer. It is the heartbeat of our relationship with God and one of the ways we experience His presence, His voice, and His power. Just as the body cannot live without breath, the believer cannot thrive without prayer. It is through prayer that we connect with the heart of God, and it is through prayer that we see heaven touch earth.

The power of prayer is not found in the eloquence of our words or the length of time we spend praying, but in the sincerity of our hearts and the intimacy we build with God. Prayer is not a ritual to be performed but a relationship to be nurtured. It is in those quiet moments of prayer that we begin to see God's hand move in our lives and the lives of others. When we pray, we align ourselves with God's purposes, and our lives become conduits for His will to be done.

Throughout Scripture, we see the undeniable power of prayer. From the prayers of Moses, who interceded on behalf of Israel, to the fervent prayers of Jesus in Gethsemane, prayer has always been the vehicle for divine intervention. The same power that raised the dead, healed the sick, and brought nations to their knees is available to us through prayer. This power is not reserved for a select few but is accessible to every believer who seeks God with a humble heart.

Prayer is a significant catalyst for deeper intimacy with God. It draws us closer to His heart and gives us access to His thoughts, desires, and plans. The more time we spend in prayer, the more we begin to understand God's will for our lives. Prayer opens the door to a deeper relationship with Him, one that transcends the surface level and moves us into profound closeness. In prayer, we are invited to listen as much as we speak, allowing God's voice to shape our hearts and direct our steps.

Prayer is also the spark that ignites revival. Every great move of God throughout history has been birthed in prayer. Whether in personal revival—where hearts are awakened to the love and call of God—or corporate revival that spreads across nations, prayer has always been the foundation. It is through prayer that we ask God to awaken our spirits, revive our communities, and heal our land. Without prayer, revival cannot happen. But when we pray, we invite the breath of God to move among us and bring life to what was once dead.

Oswald Chambers once said: Prayer is the vital breath of the Christian; not the thing that makes him alive, but the evidence that he is alive.

Never undervalue prayer. It is an open tap to a never-ending supply of spiritual power. When we pray, we are tapping into the unlimited resources of heaven. Prayer is like the wheel that releases the floodgates of heaven. Through prayer, we gain the strength to face spiritual battles, the wisdom to make God-honoring decisions, and the courage to walk in obedience to His Word. Prayer gives us access to the power of the Holy Spirit, enabling us to live victoriously in a world filled with challenges and temptations. It equips us to stand firm in faith and be vessels of God's power and presence in the world.

"Your anointing has made me strong and mighty. You've empowered my life for triumph by pouring fresh oil over me." (Psalm 92:10, TPT)

One prayer once in your life will not keep you filled up. One full tank when you buy a car can get you far, but not that far. When my car has an empty fuel tank a visit to the petrol station is the only thing that will work. I can do a hundred other good things, have great intentions to go and a pocket full of money to buy more petrol, but my tank will still be empty until I go to the petrol station. You must go to prayer and be filled often. God's Holy Spirit is His fuel station that never runs dry, but it is not automatic. You have to get up to get filled.

As we move into Part two, *The Power of Prayer*, we will explore how prayer transforms our relationship with God, fuels spiritual revival, and empowers us to live out our faith with boldness. This journey is an invitation to go deeper, to see prayer not as an obligation but as an incredible opportunity to commune with the living God. In every season, prayer is our lifeline—it is the foundation of a life fully surrendered to Him.

4

Going Higher Through Prayer

Jeremiah 33:3 (NKJV) - "Call to Me and I will answer you and show you great and mighty things."

Prayer is a personal conversation with God, but it is also so much more. It is the intimate connection of your heart, mind, and soul with your Creator, reaching out to Him with your words, your thoughts, your very being. Prayer can be formal or informal, silent or loud, a deep pouring out of your heart to the One who knows it best. And through prayer, God reveals His plans, drawing you into the purpose He has designed just for you.

Prayer is both our tool and our weapon. It is a force the enemy cannot touch, a power that's unstoppable. When we pray, we tap into a source that conquers every fear and every challenge.

Look at Jesus. His life and ministry were grounded in prayer. No matter how busy He was, no matter the demands or pressures on Him, He always made time to connect with the Father. If Jesus, the Son of God, needed that time in prayer, how much more do we need it?

True prayer begins with belief. Belief in a personal God who listens, who responds, who is active in every detail of our lives. When we believe this, prayer becomes an experience, not just a task. *"My sheep listen to my voice",* Jesus says in John 10:27. Without prayer, we miss His voice, His guidance, and His presence. To know Him, to experience the fullness of His love, we must build our relationship with Him—continually, intentionally.

Your prayer life reflects the health of your relationship with God. Without it, you are powerless. Prayer must be a priority, not an afterthought. Prayer is a verb. It is something we do. Jesus often prayed through the night, finding solitude with the Father. If He valued that connection, how can we afford not to?

An acceptable prayer is one offered from a heart fully engaged, vulnerable, and open before God. It is recognizing His presence, responding to His movements, and surrendering to His will. This level of intimacy cannot be taught—it's caught, it's felt, it's experienced. There is a place in the spirit where you lose yourself in worship, where God meets you in profound ways. Psalm 91:1-2 (NKJV) says, *"He that dwells in the secret place of the Most High will abide under the shadow of the Almighty."*

This journey is about submission, surrendering every part of your life to God. Intimacy with Him deepens as we lay down our own plans and desires. The more we submit, the deeper we experience Him.

Pray with a Sincere Heart

Come to God with authenticity. There is no need for pretenses or masks in prayer. God already knows every corner of your heart. He sees your doubts, your fears, and your struggles. So be honest. Lay it all out before Him.

When you come to God in prayer, share everything, raw and unfiltered. When you pray sincerely, your relationship with God becomes deeper, richer, and more intimate. This honesty brings transformation, because God meets us where we truly are, not where we pretend to be.

In that authenticity, your heart, mind, and soul come together, aligned and fully present before Him. There is no need to hold anything back, because God desires a real, vulnerable connection with you. He is not looking for perfect words; He is looking for an open heart.

Pray with Faith

Faith grows when you talk to God! Approach God with confidence, standing firm in the promises He has given you. Faith in prayer is the assurance that God hears you and moves in response to your petitions. Hebrews 11:6 tells us that *"without faith it is impossible to please God."* Your faith fuels your prayers, turning them into powerful declarations of God's truth.

When you pray, let your faith guide your words. Remind yourself of the truth in God's Word, because the prayers of the righteous are powerful and effective. Even when you do not see an immediate answer, trust that God is working. He hears the cries of His people and delights in answering. Pray with the confidence that God will always respond because He is faithful to His promises.

The Gospel is a reminder that you can boldly approach God because of what Jesus has done. His death and resurrection have removed every barrier, every ounce of guilt and condemnation. Because of Jesus, you do not have to hide in shame or doubt your worth. You can come boldly to the throne of grace, as Hebrews 4:16 says, and find mercy and help in your time of need.

As you pray, remember the cross and the power of the Holy Spirit at work in you. The enemy will try to convince you that you are unworthy, that you do not belong in God's presence. But you have been redeemed, restored, and made new through Jesus' sacrifice. Do not let anything keep you from coming to God with confidence. Know that Jesus has already paved the way for you to have a deep, abiding relationship with the Father.

Prayer Is About Surrender

Prayer, at its core, is surrender. It is saying, *"Not my will, but Yours, be done."* It is releasing control and letting God lead. As Jesus prayed in

Gethsemane, He surrendered His will to the Father's plan. To enter into a deep, intimate relationship with God, you must lay down your desires, trusting that God's will is better than anything you could imagine.

Prayer is not about changing God's mind; it's about letting Him change yours. It is about aligning your heart with His, allowing Him to mould you into the person He is calling you to be. Every time you pray, you are participating in what God is doing. He gets the glory, and you get the privilege of walking with Him, growing closer to Him with each step. In prayer, you discover who He is—and in discovering Him, you discover who you were created to be.

Through prayer, you are on a journey of discovering God's heart, His character, and His love for you. And as you do, you will uncover the truth about yourself, your purpose, and the life He is inviting you to live. This is prayer—divine communication with God that transforms, uplifts, and leads you into a life of abundance.

Through prayer, we are invited to step into a new realm where God's voice becomes clearer, where His plans unfold, and where our understanding of life shifts. When God says in Jeremiah 33:3 (NKJV), *"Call to Me and I will answer you and show you great and mighty things,"* He is opening the door to revelation. He is promising to show us things we could never know without seeking Him.

When we pray, we are lifted into heavenly places. It is as if our feet are still on the ground, but our hearts and spirits are caught up in the presence of God. In these moments of communion with Him, we gain a glimpse of His higher perspective. The things that seem impossible, the situations that feel overwhelming, begin to shift when we see them from His vantage point. Our circumstances do not necessarily change immediately, but our perspective does. And that makes all the difference.

The power of prayer is not found in our eloquence or in the length of time we spend praying. It is found in the posture of our hearts. When we approach God with a heart that seeks Him, we find that He is already waiting to show us "great and mighty things." Prayer is an invitation to come closer, to rise above the limitations of our earthly view and step into the higher plans of God. As we ascend through prayer, we leave behind the distractions and noise that keep us grounded in the chaos of the world. We are lifted, not physically, but spiritually, into a place where we can see with clarity, wisdom, and peace.

A Higher Calling in Prayer

From the mountaintop encounters of Moses to the apostle John being called to look into heavenly realities in the book of Revelation, there's a consistent theme: God invites His people to rise above their normal limits. In Revelation 4:1 (NKJV), God says to John, *"Come up here, and I will show you things which must take place..."* This invitation was not only for John, it is for *anyone* who longs to see more of God's plans and purposes.

Prayer is our "come to me" moment. Every time we enter into prayer, we are responding to God's call to ascend, to see beyond what is right in front of us. It is a powerful invitation to leave behind the distractions and worries that cloud our vision and step into a place of intimacy where God's voice becomes the loudest. The higher we go in prayer, the more we begin to understand that life's answers are not found in the chaos below but in the quiet, elevated space of God's presence.

There is something about going higher that changes us. When we seek God through prayer, we are no longer content with living life from a ground-level view. God invites us to step into His perspective, to see things the way He does. From this place, we begin to see what is truly important, what is eternal. Our priorities shift. The things that once weighed us down do not seem so heavy when we have ascended into God's presence.

This higher calling is not just about personal revelation or insight. It is about transformation. Prayer lifts us out of our own limited thinking and places us in alignment with God's will. In prayer, we are not just talking to God about our desires, we are listening for His. We are allowing our hearts to be shaped by His thoughts, our lives to be moved by

His purposes. This is why prayer is so much more than a routine. It is a life-altering, perspective-shifting encounter with the Almighty.

Elevation Through Prayer

The act of prayer lifts us higher. It elevates not just our spirits, but our understanding.

Often, we come to God weighed down by the burdens of life—uncertainties, fears, or decisions that need to be made. But when we step into prayer, something remarkable happens. Our focus shifts. Instead of being consumed by the issues before us, we begin to see things through the lens of eternity. We stop looking at our problems and start looking at the God who is above them all.

Colossians 3:1-2 encourages us to set our hearts and minds on things above, not on earthly things. This is exactly what happens in prayer. We are invited to rise above the immediate concerns and fix our gaze on heavenly realities. In doing so, we gain clarity, insight, and peace. Prayer does not always change our circumstances right away, but it changes how we see them. And that can be the difference between despair and hope, between anxiety and trust.

Think about the times when you have felt overwhelmed, when life seemed to be closing in on all sides. Then you prayed. The situation might not have changed right away, but something inside of you did. Your spirit lifted. Your heart found peace. Your hope for an answer and a breakthrough rises within you. That is what prayer does. It gives us access to a perspective that transcends our own. The higher we go in prayer, the less weight we carry, and the more we trust that God is in control.

This elevation through prayer is not merely about seeing things differently. It is about being transformed. As we ascend, our minds are renewed, and our hearts are strengthened. The things that once seemed insurmountable no longer have the same power over us. We have seen from God's view, and it changes everything.

Revelation in the Presence of God

One of the greatest blessings of prayer is revelation. God does not just hear our prayers, He responds by showing us things we could never discover on our own. When God says in Jeremiah 33:3, *"Call to Me and I will answer you and show you great and mighty things,"* He is promising to reveal the hidden things, the mysteries that we can only access through prayer.

These revelations are not always immediate, but they are transformative. There are moments in prayer when God speaks directly to our hearts, giving us wisdom for decisions, comfort in times of grief, and direction for the path ahead. Other times, the revelation may come quietly, over time, as we continue to seek Him. But make no mistake—when we seek God in prayer, we are stepping into a place where divine mysteries are revealed.

Moses experienced this on Mount Sinai. It was there, in the presence of God, that he received the Ten Commandments, the divine blueprint for how God's people should live. He was not given this revelation while surrounded by the noise and chaos of daily life. He had to ascend the mountain, leaving behind the distractions, to hear from God. In the same way, we must enter into the secret place of prayer if we want to receive revelation from God. The higher we go in prayer, the more we are able to hear His voice.

ALWAYS PRAY in the Spirit on all occasions with all kinds of prayers and requests. With this in mind, be alert and keep praying for all the Lord's people. (Ephesians 6:18, emphasis added)

Are you prepared for revival or survival? Most people POST-pray giving no room for God to prepare them for what is happening until it has happened. These are survival prayers and not revival prayers. Jesus always PRE-prayed. He prayed before things happened and that is why He was always ready with faith and power to release revival in every place He went.

This revelation is not just for our own personal benefit. Often, what God reveals in prayer is meant to be shared, to impact the lives of others.

When we ascend in prayer, we become carriers of God's heart for the world. We begin to understand His purposes, not just for ourselves but for those around us. Prayer is the birthplace of vision, of strategy, and of direction. It is where God's plans are revealed to His people.

Prayer is not passive. It is an active engagement with God's presence and His power. When we pray, we are entering into a place of divine partnership, where God moves on our behalf. The higher we go in prayer, the more we access the power of God to bring change. Whether it is in our personal lives, our families, or our communities, prayer has the power to shift circumstances and transform hearts.

In Ephesians 6:12, we are reminded that the battles we face are not against flesh and blood but against spiritual forces. We fight these battles in prayer. The higher we ascend in prayer, the more equipped we are to stand firm in the face of spiritual opposition. Prayer gives us access to the resources of heaven. We do not fight with our own strength; we fight with the power of God.

The power that raised Christ from the dead is available to us when we pray. We are not left to face life's challenges alone. Through prayer, we tap into the supernatural power of God. It is this power that strengthens us in times of weakness, gives us wisdom when we do not know what to do, and grants us peace when everything around us feels chaotic. The more we ascend through prayer, the more we are able to carry this power into every area of our lives.

Prayer is not just a time to speak to God, it is a time to be empowered by Him. As we draw near, He fills us with His Spirit, equipping us for the challenges ahead. The higher we go in prayer, the more He transforms us, and the more we are able to bring heaven to earth.

5

The Prayer Of Intimacy

Matthew 6:6 - "But when you pray, go into your room, close the door and pray to your Father, who is unseen."

Prayer is the gateway to intimacy with God.

In its most personal and quiet moments, prayer draws us closer, allowing us to experience a relationship with God that goes beyond words and actions. Jesus, in Matthew 6:6, invites us into this secret place: *"When you pray, go into your room, close the door and pray to your Father, who is unseen."* The secret place of prayer is not just about being physically alone, it is about entering a space where nothing competes for your heart but God. It is here, in the stillness, that true intimacy is cultivated.

There are no substitutes for this secret place. No quick methods or spiritual shortcuts can replicate the depth that comes from time spent alone with God. It is where the noise of life fades and the voice of God becomes clear. In this space, our relationship with Him deepens as we pour out our hearts, not in formalities but in raw honesty. It is here that we are known fully and can know God in a way that transforms us from the inside out.

The Secret Place of Prayer

The secret place is not a physical location, although for many of us, it is helpful to find a quiet space. The secret place is the internal sanctuary where you meet with God. It is a place set apart in your heart and mind, where the distractions of the world are left behind. There, you are free to be yourself—no pretence, no masks—just you and God. This kind of prayer is not public, not for show, but deeply personal.

Jesus emphasised this when He spoke of closing the door. The imagery of closing the door goes beyond merely finding a private room. It speaks to shutting out everything that would compete for your attention. In the secret place, we learn to focus solely on God, giving Him our undivided attention. Our prayers are no longer just a list of requests but a conversation between us and our Creator.

It is in this space that intimacy with God is built.

The more time we spend in the secret place, the more we grow in our knowledge of Him and experience His presence in our lives. It is a relationship that deepens with every moment spent in communion. And just like any relationship, intimacy with God requires time and attention. The more intentional we are about seeking Him in prayer, the more our hearts align with His.

Some days, entering this space may feel like an uphill battle. Life's distractions and burdens can make it hard to focus. But those are the days when intimacy with God is most needed. In the quiet of prayer, we lay down our worries, doubts, and fears, exchanging them for His peace, His wisdom, and His strength. The more we practice entering into this secret place, the more natural it becomes.

A Conversation with God

Prayer, at its heart, is conversation. Always remember, it is a *dialogue*, not a *monologue*. Too often, we treat prayer as a list of things we need from God or a routine we go through to check a box. But intimacy with God comes when we stop talking long enough to listen. In the secret place, there is time and space to hear from God, to wait in His presence, and to allow Him to speak to our hearts.

Think about the closest relationships in your life. They are built through time spent together, through listening as much as speaking. Prayer is no different. God invites us to bring our concerns, our joys, and our needs before Him, but He also invites to be still and know that He is God. In those moments of stillness, God often speaks the loudest. His voice may not always be audible, but we can deeply feel His impressions, His peace, and His guidance.

As we grow in intimacy with Him, our prayers become less about getting things from God and more about simply being with Him.

Sometimes the most intimate moments with God are those when words fail us. When we sit in His presence, without knowing what to say, trusting that He understands even the groans of our hearts. Romans 8:26 tells us that the Holy Spirit intercedes for us with groanings too deep for words. In these moments, God meets us in our vulnerability, and it is in our weakness that His strength is made perfect.

There is a depth to prayer that cannot be reached without surrender. True intimacy with God requires that we open every part of our hearts to Him, even the parts we would rather keep hidden. But in the secret place, there is no hiding. There is only openness and vulnerability. And that is where we find the beauty of intimacy with God. He already knows every part of us, but He waits for us to willingly lay it all before Him.

The prayer of intimacy is not about formality or routine. It is about relationship. It's about allowing ourselves to be fully seen and fully loved by God. And in turn, it is about knowing Him in ways that transform how we live, how we love, and how we pray. The more intimate our relationship with God becomes, the more our prayers reflect His heart rather than just our own desires. We begin to pray His will, not because we feel we have to, but because we have come to know and trust Him deeply.

This kind of intimacy does not happen overnight. It is cultivated through time, through consistency, and through the daily decision to come closer. Just as with any relationship, intimacy with God takes intentionality. We must make room for it in our busy lives, prioritising time in the secret place over everything else that clamours for our attention.

God is always calling us to go deeper. No matter how close we feel we are, there is always more. More of His love, more of His presence, more of His wisdom. The prayer of intimacy is an invitation to explore the depths of God's heart, to go beyond surface-level conversations and dive into the richness of knowing Him fully. It is in these deeper places of prayer that we find the fullness of joy spoken of in Psalm 16:11 (NKJV): *"In Your presence is fullness of joy; at Your right hand are pleasures forevermore."*

God never rebukes us for wanting more of Him. In fact, He invites it. The more we desire Him, the more He reveals Himself. But this depth comes with a cost—it requires surrender. It requires that we let go of our need for control and trust Him completely. It requires that we come to Him with no agenda, no pretence, but simply with a heart that longs to know Him more.

And in those moments when we do surrender, when we lay aside our own desires for the sake of knowing Him, we experience a depth of intimacy that changes everything. It changes how we see ourselves, how we see others, and how we see the world. It gives us eyes to see from a heavenly perspective, ears to hear His voice, and hearts that are aligned with His will.

The challenge for many is not entering the secret place but staying there. Life has a way of pulling us back into busyness and distraction. But the secret to cultivating lasting intimacy with God is remaining in the secret place, even as we go about our daily lives. It is possible to carry the presence of God with you wherever you go. The secret place of prayer becomes less of a location and more of a posture of the heart.

Jesus Himself modelled this. Throughout His ministry, He often withdrew to solitary places to pray, but He also carried the presence of His Father with Him at all times. He lived in constant communion with God. That is the example we are called to follow. To make prayer and intimacy with God not just a part of our day, but the foundation of how we live.

Remaining in the secret place means cultivating a lifestyle of prayer. It means that even in the busyness of life, we take moments to turn our hearts toward God, to breathe a prayer, to listen for His voice. It means that we never fully leave the secret place, because it has become a part of who we are.

Every time we enter the secret place of prayer, God invites us to go deeper. Every moment spent with Him reveals something new, something more profound. The prayer of intimacy is not about mastering a technique or following a formula, it is about *relationship*. It is about knowing God in the deepest way possible and allowing that relationship to shape every part of our lives.

There will always be more of God to discover. He is infinite, and His love for us is without limit. As we continue to seek Him in the secret place, He draws us into a relationship that is ever-growing, ever-deepening. It is a journey that will take a lifetime, but one that is worth every moment.

So, as you step into the secret place, know that you are answering an invitation from the Creator of the universe to come closer, to know Him more fully, and to experience the depth of His love.

The prayer of intimacy is not a duty, it is a gift. And in that gift, you will find life, joy, and the very heart of God.

6

Intercession—Birthing Revival

Acts 1:14 - "They all joined together constantly in prayer…"

Throughout history, revival has always been birthed in the prayer room. Every great move of God, every outpouring of His Spirit, and every transformation of a people or nation has started with one thing: *fervent, persistent, unified prayer.*

In Acts 1:14, we read, *"They all joined together constantly in prayer…"* This was a committed, intentional time of intercession where the early believers poured out their hearts before God, asking Him to move.

And move He did.

Prayer is the furnace where the flames of revival are ignited. Before the world sees a demonstration of God's power, it begins with individuals and groups coming together in the secret place, crying out for more of Him. Revival does not start on stages or platforms. It is birthed in the quiet, unseen places where God's people refuse to relent until they see Him move.

The upper room in Acts is the blueprint for this truth. Those who gathered there had no idea how or when God would fulfil His promise, but they knew one thing: they had to pray. So, they waited. They prayed. They stayed in that place of intercession until heaven responded with fire. What came next changed the world forever—Pentecost, the outpouring of the Holy Spirit. But it did not come without that time of persistent prayer.

Every revival follows the same pattern. Before the fire of God falls, His people must first be found on their knees.

Intercession is not for the faint of heart. It is not something we engage in when it's convenient or when we feel like it. True intercession is marked by persistence. It is a labour of love, a spiritual travail that demands our hearts be fully engaged. Revival is birthed when we press into prayer with everything we have, refusing to give up, no matter how long it takes.

The Welsh Revival of 1904 is a powerful example. It began when a small group of believers, led by Evan Roberts, made a commitment to pray until they saw God move. They did not set a time limit on their prayers. They didn't pray for a day or a week and then stop if nothing happened. No, they prayed until heaven broke through. And it did. The revival that followed swept through Wales like wildfire, touching every aspect of society and bringing thousands to Christ.

But it did not happen overnight. Revival never does.

Revival is the result of sustained, fervent intercession—prayer that says, *"We will not stop until we see God move."* It is this kind of prayer that touches the heart of God and opens the door for Him to pour out His Spirit.

Revival Begins in the Heart

Everyone wants a revival that comes with a sudden unannounced supernatural outpouring, but that is not how it has ever happened. Yes, to some it may have looked that way, but before revival can touch a nation, it must first touch the hearts of those willing to wait in the secret place. Revival is looking for intercessors. As we pray, God begins to work on our hearts, aligning them with His. He shows us where we need to repent, where we need deeper surrender and where we must pull down other high things.

This personal revival is where it all starts.

You cannot birth revival in your church, your city, or your nation if it has not first been birthed in your own heart. It begins when we humble ourselves before God, seeking His face with all our hearts, asking Him to move not just around us, but within us. As He changes us, as we are set ablaze with His presence, that fire begins to spread. Revival starts in the heart and moves outward, touching everything and everyone in its path.

Many people want to see revival, but few are willing to pay the price of persistent, personal intercession. But history shows us that those who are willing to labor in prayer, to push past the distractions and the discouragement, are the ones who see the greatest moves of God.

The Power of Unity in Prayer

Revival is birthed when believers come together in unity, seeking God with one heart and one mind. The early church understood this. Acts 1:14 tells us that they *"joined together constantly in prayer."* They did not pray in isolation. They prayed together. And it was in that place of unified prayer that God poured out His Spirit.

The Azusa Street Revival, which began in 1906, is another powerful example of this. People from all walks of life—different races, denominations, and backgrounds—gathered in a small, humble mission to seek God together. There was no agenda, no program—just a hunger for God and a commitment to pray until He moved.

And move He did.

What followed was one of the greatest revivals in history, with countless lives transformed and the Pentecostal movement birthed.

There is something powerful that happens when believers come together in prayer. Jesus Himself said, *"For where two or three gather in My name, there am I with them"* (Matthew 18:20). Revival is birthed when the people of God unite in prayer, setting aside their differences and focusing on one thing—seeking His face. It is in that place of unity that the heavens are opened, and God moves in ways we cannot even begin to imagine.

The Fire of God

Revival is often described as a fire. It spreads quickly, igniting everything in its path. But for that fire to start, there must first be a spark. That spark is intercession. Without it, the fire cannot burn. The fire of revival is sparked in the prayer room, and it is sustained by ongoing, fervent prayer. Once the fire begins to burn, it is our responsibility to keep it burning through continued intercession. This is a fire you stoke so that you are never left out in the cold!

The revivals of old, whether in Wales, Azusa Street, or the Great Awakening, all started with that spark of prayer. People who were willing to lay down their lives, to dedicate themselves to prayer, ignited a flame that spread across nations. But even after the fire was lit, it had to be tended. Revival does not sustain itself. It must be fueled by the continuous prayers of God's people.

Paul said we should pray without ceasing! [1 Thessalonians 5:16-18] In the Old Testament, the responsibility to keep the fire always burning fell upon the priests. In the New Testament we are the priests tasked with the responsibility of keeping God's fire burning in our hearts. One of the ways that the priests of old kept the fire always burning on the altar was to bring a consistent offering. If a fire does not have fuel, it does not burn!

Leviticus 6:13 says, *"The fire must be kept burning on the altar continuously; it must not go out."* This is true of revival as well. Once God begins to move, we cannot sit back and relax. We must continue to intercede, to pray, to ask God for more. Revival is sustained by the same prayer that birthed it. If we want to see the fire of revival continue to burn, we must remain on our knees.

The Cost of Revival

Revival always comes at a cost. It costs time, energy, and often, great personal sacrifice. Those who have experienced revival firsthand will tell you that it is not convenient. It is messy. It disrupts the status quo. But it is worth every cost, every sacrifice, because when God moves, everything changes.

The revival at Asbury College in 1970 is a powerful reminder of this. What began as a simple chapel service turned into a week-long outpouring of the Holy Spirit that spread across the campus and beyond. But it did not happen without a cost. Students and faculty sacrificed their time, their schedules, their plans, to stay in the presence of God. They prayed day and night, asking God to continue moving, and He did. The result was a revival that touched thousands of lives.

Revival requires a willingness to lay down our agendas, to be inconvenienced, to spend hours in prayer when we would rather be doing something else. It requires us to be fully surrendered to God, willing to do whatever it takes to see His kingdom come.

Revival in Our Generation

We stand at the threshold of revival. The signs are all around us. People are hungry for more of God. The world is desperate for hope, for healing, for something real. But if we want to see revival in our generation, we must be willing to pay the price. We must be willing to labor in prayer, to intercede until we see God move.

Revival is not a distant dream. It is the heart of God for His people. He desires to pour out His Spirit in ways we have never seen before. But He is waiting for His people to rise up in intercession, to cry out for revival with a desperation that will not be denied.

The question is, are we willing to pay the price? Are we willing to be the generation that births revival through prayer?

The answer lies in our willingness to get on our knees, to join together in unity, and to pray until we see heaven break through.

Part Three - Revival

Revival stirs the deepest parts of our soul, awakening us to holiness, repentance, and the overwhelming presence of God. It is a profound movement that transforms hearts and lives. When revival comes, it ignites a desire for righteousness, a return to God's ways, and a hunger for His Spirit like never before.

At the heart of revival is a call to holiness. This is not a superficial change but a deep, inward transformation. It is a movement that turns people away from complacency and sin, calling them back to a life that reflects God's purity. Revival compels us to examine our hearts, leading us to genuine repentance, a repentance that moves beyond words to a complete turning of our lives toward God's will and His ways.

The manifest presence of God is the hallmark of revival. When God's Spirit moves, it is undeniable. There is a tangible weight of His glory that falls, transforming not only individual lives but entire communities. Revival is marked by this divine encounter, where people experience God in ways that leave them forever changed. It is an awakening that touches every corner of our lives, calling us to live with passion, purpose, and a deeper connection to His heart.

As we step into this part of the journey, prepare yourself for the transformational power that revival brings. This is the time when God's Spirit moves in ways that shift the atmosphere, bringing life, restoration, and a renewed hunger for His presence.

7

What is Revival?

Psalm 85:6 - "Will You not revive us again, that Your people may rejoice in You?"

Revival is a powerful movement of God that brings life to what was dead, a stirring of the soul that brings people back to God with a renewed sense of purpose and passion. It is a divine moment when God breathes His Spirit into hearts, families, communities, and even nations, awakening them from spiritual slumber. Psalm 85:6 captures this cry: *"Will You not revive us again, that Your people may rejoice in You?"* It is a plea for God to come and refresh, renew, and restore His people.

But what exactly is revival? To understand its significance, we must go beyond our modern understanding of the word. Revival is not simply an emotional high or a series of exciting church services. It is not just an event with loud music, charismatic preaching, or filled altars. True revival is a move of God that transforms lives, purges sin, and awakens a deep hunger for holiness. It brings repentance, renewal, and awakening, all of which lead to a deeper relationship with God and a lasting impact on the world around us.

Defining Revival

The word "revival" comes from the Latin word *revivere*, meaning "to live again." It implies a restoration of life, vigor, and vitality. Biblically, revival occurs when God's people are spiritually renewed and brought back to life. It is about returning to our first love, rekindling the fire of devotion that may have grown cold over time. Revival is about restoring what has been lost and reclaiming the fullness of God's purpose for His people.

In Psalm 85, the psalmist pleads with God for revival, recognizing that without His intervention, His people remain stagnant and lifeless. This is the essence of biblical revival, a divine restoration that only God can bring. It is a supernatural move that begins in the hearts of His people and spreads outward, touching every aspect of life. It is God's way of drawing us closer to Him, renewing our hearts, and preparing us for His greater purposes.

Throughout the Bible, we see moments of revival when God's people turned back to Him after periods of rebellion or spiritual apathy. These moments were always marked by repentance, prayer, and a hunger for holiness. In Nehemiah 8, after the people rebuilt the walls of Jerusalem, Ezra gathered them to read the Law, and as they heard the Word, their hearts were pierced. They wept, repented, and committed themselves anew to God's covenant. This was revival, a return to God's ways, a deep conviction of sin, and a renewed commitment to live according to His Word.

Revival Begins with Repentance

At the heart of every true revival is repentance. Without it, there can be no revival. Whatever we have in our lives that hinders our ascension into heavenly places must be removed. Every roadblock, wall and dark hole must be removed so that holiness can become a landing place for revival. Repentance is not simply feeling bad about sin or making a surface-level apology. It is a complete turning away from sin and a turning toward God. It requires action. It is a change of heart, mind, and action.

It is a deep sorrow for how we have strayed from God's ways and a desire to walk in holiness once again.

In Acts 3:19 (NKJV), Peter calls the people to *"Repent therefore, and be converted, that your sins may be blotted out, so that times of refreshing may come from the presence of the Lord."* True revival always begins with a recognition of our need for God and a realization that we cannot continue in our sin. When we humble ourselves and repent, we open the door for God's refreshing to flow into our lives.

Repentance is both personal and corporate. On a personal level, we must each examine our own hearts, confess our sins, and turn back to God. But revival also requires a corporate repentance, a recognition that, as a body of believers, we have drifted from God's purposes. Revival often comes when the church collectively humbles itself before God, confesses its failures, and seeks His face once again.

In 2 Chronicles 7:14 (NKJV), God gives a clear promise: *"If My people who are called by My name will humble themselves, and pray and seek My face, and turn from their wicked ways, then I will hear from heaven, and will forgive their sin and heal their land."* This is the biblical formula for revival—humility, prayer, seeking God, and repentance. When these elements are present, God promises to respond with healing, forgiveness, and restoration.

Renewal and Revival

Revival means being renewed by God's Spirit. Renewal is the process by which God restores what we have lost, reviving our passion for Him, reigniting our love for His Word, and renewing our commitment to His mission. In revival, God breathes new life into His people, awakening them from spiritual slumber and empowering them to live out their faith with boldness and conviction.

Isaiah 40:31 (NKJV) gives us a picture of this renewal: *"But those who wait on the Lord shall renew their strength; they shall mount up with wings like eagles, they shall run and not be weary, they shall walk and not faint."* In the place of waiting, of seeking God and depending on

Him, He renews our strength. God gives us fresh energy, fresh vision, and fresh passion to carry out the work He has called us to do.

This renewal is not something we can manufacture on our own. It is a work of the Holy Spirit, who comes to refresh and revive us when we are willing to humble ourselves and seek His face. Just as a dry and barren land cannot produce fruit without rain, so our hearts cannot bear fruit without the refreshing rain of God's Spirit.

Throughout history, every revival has been marked by this kind of renewal. The Welsh Revival, led by Evan Roberts in 1904, is a powerful example. Roberts and a small group of believers began to pray fervently for God to move, and as they prayed, the Spirit of God began to fall on them. God renewed their hearts, transformed their lives, and the fire of revival spread throughout Wales, touching every corner of society. But it all began with a deep hunger for God and a willingness to be renewed by His Spirit.

Revival is an Awakening

Another key aspect of revival is awakening. Revival awakens us to the reality of God's presence and power. It opens our eyes to see Him more clearly, to hear His voice more distinctly, and to experience His glory in ways we have never known before. It is an awakening to His holiness, an awakening to His love, and an awakening to His purposes.

In Isaiah 60:1, the prophet declares: *"Arise, shine, for your light has come, and the glory of the Lord rises upon you."* Revival is an awakening to the glory of God. It is a moment when the light of His presence shines on us, dispelling the darkness and revealing His truth. It is an awakening that stirs our souls, causing us to rise up and take hold of all that God has for us.

This awakening is not just for the church, it is for the world. When revival comes, it awakens not only believers but also those who are far from God. It opens their eyes to the reality of His love, His grace, and His power. It brings conviction of sin and draws them into the kingdom of God.

Revival is the spark that sets the world ablaze with the fire of God's love. It's the catalyst for change, the beginning of a spiritual awakening that transforms entire communities. When revival comes, people who were once indifferent to God are suddenly awakened to their need for Him. Those who were far off are brought near, and those who were blind now see.

The Fruit of Revival

True revival always produces fruit. It is not a fleeting emotional experience but a lasting transformation that bears fruit in the lives of individuals, churches, and communities. The fruit of revival includes a deeper love for God, a greater passion for His Word, a renewed commitment to prayer, and a heart for evangelism.

In Galatians 5:22-23, Paul describes the fruit of the Spirit: *"But the fruit of the Spirit is love, joy, peace, forbearance, kindness, goodness, faithfulness, gentleness and self-control."* When revival comes, this fruit becomes evident in the lives of God's people. We begin to walk in greater love, joy, and peace. We become more patient, kind, and faithful. Our lives are marked by gentleness and self-control, and we reflect the character of Jesus in everything we do.

But the fruit of revival does not stop with individual transformation. It spills over into the church and the community. Churches that experience revival become centres of God's presence, where people encounter His love and power in tangible ways. The Gospel is preached and lived out with boldness and conviction, transforming communities. Revival brings reconciliation, healing, and restoration to broken relationships, families, and cities.

A Call to Revival

The cry for revival is a deep, heartfelt plea for God to move in power, to bring His people back to life, and to awaken the world to His presence. As we seek revival, we are asking God to do what only He can do—revive us, renew us, and awaken us to His glory.

Psalm 85:6 asks the question: *"Will You not revive us again, that Your people may rejoice in You?"* The answer is yes. God longs to revive His people. He longs to pour out His Spirit, to refresh our hearts, and to awaken us to His purposes. But revival begins with us. It begins with a humble heart, a repentant spirit, and a deep desire for more of God.

Will we respond to His call?

8

The Role of Holiness in Revival

1 Peter 1:16 (NKJV) - "Be holy, for I am holy."

Revival and holiness are inseparable. You cannot speak of one without the other, for holiness is the very atmosphere in which revival is sparked and sustained. When God calls His people into revival, He is simultaneously calling them to a deeper, more profound level of personal holiness. As it says in 1 Peter 1:16 (NKJV), *"Be holy, for I am holy."* This is an invitation to step into the fullness of who God is, into a life that mirrors His character and reflects His glory.

Holiness is often misunderstood. Some see it as rigid rule-following or moral perfection like what we see of the Pharisees in the Gospels, but holiness is so much more than our outward behavior. It is about a heart fully surrendered to God, set apart for His purposes, and devoted to living in alignment with His will. True holiness begins with an inward transformation and manifests outwardly in the way we live, love, and worship. Without holiness, we cannot hope to experience the depth of revival that God desires for us.

Holiness as the Foundation of Revival

Revival is not merely an emotional experience, but it is a spiritual awakening that brings deep, lasting change. And that change must begin with holiness. Holiness prepares the ground for revival by purifying our hearts, cleansing our minds, and aligning our lives with God's truth. Before the fire of revival can fall, God's people must be ready to receive it, and that readiness comes through holiness.

The prophet Isaiah experienced this firsthand when he encountered the holiness of God in a vision. In Isaiah 6:1-5, he describes seeing the Lord seated on a throne, high and exalted, with the train of His robe filling the temple. Seraphim surrounded Him, calling out, *"Holy, holy, holy is the Lord Almighty; the whole earth is full of His glory!"* Isaiah's immediate response was one of deep conviction and repentance. *"Woe to me!"* he cried. *"I am ruined! For I am a man of unclean lips, and I live among a people of unclean lips, and my eyes have seen the King, the Lord Almighty."*

Isaiah's vision is a powerful reminder that holiness is the foundation upon which revival is built. When we come face to face with the holiness of God, we are undone by the reality of our own sin and brokenness. But in that moment of humility, God does something miraculous—He cleanses us, purifies us, and sets us apart for His purposes. Holiness is not something we achieve on our own; it is a work of grace that God does in us when we surrender to Him.

Holiness as a Posture of the Heart

Holiness is not about perfection, but about direction. It is about the posture of our hearts. Are we moving toward God, or are we moving away from Him? Holiness is the constant pursuit of God's presence, the desire to live in a way that pleases Him and reflects His character. It is about setting our hearts and minds on things above, as Colossians 3:2 instructs us, *"Set your minds on things above, not on earthly things."*

This posture of our heart is essential for revival. Why is holiness so offensive to the modern mind? It offends the modern Christian to

DENY themselves, pick up their cross and follow Jesus. [Matthew 16:24, Luke 9:23] Holiness means something is dedicated completely or set apart absolutely for special use unto God! We want ownership of all things, but ALL THINGS are not ours! Some things are God's and until we give God what's His we will not see revival.

Karl Marx said: When you take away all that is sacred there is nothing left to worship! - No wonder so many people have nothing left to revere God with. Many struggle to go to church, pray and worship because one by one they have reasoned the removal of more and more things that are sacred to God. Could this be why revivals are not as common as they should be?

Revival cannot come to a people who are divided in their loyalties or distracted by the things of the world. God is looking for hearts that are fully devoted to Him, hearts that are willing to be purified and refined by His Spirit. In James 4:8 (NKJV), we are told, *"Draw near to God, and He will draw near to you. Cleanse your hands, you sinners, and purify your hearts, you double-minded."* Holiness requires us to purify our hearts, to rid ourselves of anything that stands in the way of our relationship with God.

In the Old Testament, the priests who ministered before the Lord had to go through a process of purification before entering the temple. They could not approach God casually or with unclean hands. In the same way, we cannot expect to experience the fullness of God's presence without first being cleansed and consecrated. Revival requires us to come before God with clean hands and pure hearts, ready to be vessels of His glory.

The Cost of Holiness

Holiness comes at a cost. It requires us to lay down our desires, our ambitions, and even our comforts to pursue God's best for our lives. Jesus Himself said in Matthew 16:24 (NKJV), *"If anyone desires to come after Me, let him deny himself, take up his cross, and follow Me."* This is the essence of holiness—a life of self-denial and surrender to God's will.

It is about choosing His ways over our own, even when it's difficult or uncomfortable.

In a world that often promotes self-indulgence and instant gratification, holiness can feel like an uphill battle. But the rewards of holiness far outweigh the cost. When we choose to live holy lives, we position ourselves to experience the fullness of God's presence and power. Holiness opens the door for revival, for it is in the place of purity that God's Spirit moves most freely.

Consider the revival that broke out in the early church. In Acts 2, we see the believers gathered together in one place, praying and waiting for the promise of the Holy Spirit. These were not perfect people, but they were people who had been set apart by God, purified by His grace, and prepared for a mighty outpouring of His Spirit. And when the Holy Spirit came, it came in power, igniting a movement that would change the world forever.

The Fear of the Lord

Holiness is deeply connected to the fear of the Lord. To fear the Lord is to revere Him, to stand in awe of His majesty and holiness. It is not a fear that drives us away from God, but a fear that draws us closer to Him, recognizing His greatness and our need for Him. One could also say the fear of the Lord is any suggestion that there could be an alternative of living without God. Life without God should be the craziest thing anyone could ever come up with. Proverbs 9:10 (NKJV) tells us, *"The fear of the Lord is the beginning of wisdom, and knowledge of the Holy One is understanding."*

Revival cannot happen without the fear of the Lord. When we lose our reverence for God, we lose our sensitivity to His presence. Holiness restores that reverence, reminding us of who God is and who we are in light of Him. It humbles us, bringing us to a place of unending worship and surrender.

In the revival at Asbury College in 1970, students were overwhelmed by the fear of the Lord. As they gathered for a routine chapel service, the presence of God fell so powerfully that students began to weep, confess their sins, and repent. What was meant to be a one-hour service turned into a week-long outpouring of God's Spirit. This revival was marked by deep repentance, humility, and a renewed sense of God's holiness. It was a revival that began with the fear of the Lord.

Personal Holiness Prepares Us for Revival

Personal holiness is the soil in which revival is planted. Without holiness, our hearts are not prepared to receive the fullness, the full weight, of what God wants to do. Holiness makes room for God's presence to dwell in us and through us. It is through personal holiness that we become vessels fit for the Master's use, as Paul describes in 2 Timothy 2:21 (NKJV), *"Therefore, if anyone cleanses himself from the latter, he will be a vessel for honor, sanctified and useful for the Master, prepared for every good work."*

This cleansing is not a one-time event but a continual process. Holiness is not something we achieve and then move on from—it is a daily decision to walk in the Spirit, to die to self, and to pursue God with all our hearts. Revival requires this kind of daily surrender to purity, this ongoing commitment to live in a way that honors God.

As we pursue holiness, God begins to work in us in ways we cannot imagine. He refines us, purifies us, and prepares us for greater levels of His presence and power. Revival is not something we can manufacture or manipulate, it is the natural outflow of hearts that are fully surrendered to God, hearts that have been purified and set apart for His glory.

The Fruit of Holiness

When holiness takes root in our lives, it produces fruit that lasts. The fruit of holiness is seen in our character, our relationships, and our impact on the world around us. Galatians 5:22-23 describes the fruit of the Spirit as *"love, joy, peace, patience, kindness, goodness, faithfulness, gentleness, and self-control."* These are the markers of a life that has been transformed by God's holiness.

Revival brings with it a fresh outpouring of the fruit of the Spirit. As we are purified and made holy, we begin to reflect the character of Jesus in everything we do. Our lives become a testimony to the power of God's transforming grace. We love more deeply, forgive more freely, and serve more selflessly. This is the fruit of revival, a life that looks increasingly more like Jesus.

Holiness also produces a greater hunger for God. The more we experience His holiness, the more we desire to be in His presence. Revival fans the flames of this hunger, drawing us deeper into the heart of God and igniting a passion for His glory. It is in the place of holiness that we find true intimacy with God, for He is a holy God, and those who seek Him must do so with pure hearts.

The Call to Holiness

Revival is a call to holiness. It is a call to return to the heart of God, to be purified by His Spirit, and to live lives that reflect His glory. As we pursue holiness, we open ourselves up to the possibility of revival, not just in our own lives, but in our families, churches, and communities. Holiness is the key that unlocks the door to revival, for it is in the place of purity that God's Spirit moves most powerfully.

"Be holy, for I am holy," the Lord says. This is His invitation to us, an invitation to step into the fullness of His presence and to experience the life-transforming power of revival. Will we respond? Will we choose holiness, even when it is hard? Will we lay down our desires and ambitions for the sake of His glory?

The choice is ours. And as we choose holiness, we position ourselves to receive the revival that God so deeply desires to pour out.

9

Revival Starts with You

2 Chronicles 7:14 - "If my people, who are called by my name, will humble themselves and pray..."

Revival is often thought of as something that happens on a large scale, a sweeping move of God that shakes communities, cities, and even nations. But the truth is, revival does not begin in church services or public gatherings. It doesn't start with mass evangelistic events or large prayer meetings. Revival begins in the hearts of God's children. It starts with you, with a personal, intimate encounter with God that transforms your life from the inside out.

When God speaks in 2 Chronicles 7:14, He is calling His people to a posture of humility, prayer, and repentance. He is not addressing the crowds but His people—those who are already in covenant with Him. *"If My people, who are called by My name, will humble themselves and pray..."* This is the invitation to revival. It is not a corporate call at first; it's a personal one. Revival starts with a heart willing to be broken before God, a life laid down in humility, prayer, and obedience.

The Seed of Revival is in Your Heart

The seed of revival is planted in the soil of your heart long before it grows into a mighty tree that bears fruit for others to see. It begins in the secret place, where you meet with God alone. Just like a seed, revival must be nurtured, watered, and cultivated in your personal life before it can take root in your family, church, or community. Jesus teaches in Matthew 6:6, *"But when you pray, go into your room, close the door and pray to your Father, who is unseen. Then your Father, who sees what is done in secret, will reward you."* The revival you seek for your community starts with the secret prayers of your heart.

The revival that transforms churches and communities flows out of hearts that the Spirit of God transforms in the quiet place. The fires of revival are lit not on the platform, but in the prayer closet. It is here, in the personal, intimate moments with God, that your heart is set on fire. The fire that burns in the individual heart can then spread like wildfire, igniting those around you.

In Acts 1:14, we see this truth unfold as the early believers gathered in the upper room. They weren't seeking a public spectacle; they were simply praying together in obedience to Jesus' instruction. And in the hiddenness of that upper room, the fire of revival was birthed. It started with individual hearts in prayer and then overflowed into the streets of Jerusalem, drawing thousands to Christ.

Personal Prayer as the Catalyst for Revival

Prayer is the lifeblood of revival. Without prayer, there can be no revival, no move of God, no transformation. The Welsh Revival of 1904, for example, was born out of the fervent prayers of a small group of believers. Evan Roberts, a young man hungry for God, began to pray fervently for revival, and his personal prayers ignited a movement that swept through Wales, transforming not only churches but entire communities.

Your prayers have the power to spark a move of God in your own life and in the lives of those around you. The Bible is filled with examples of individuals who prayed for revival, and God responded. In 1 Kings 18, Elijah prayed on Mount Carmel, and God sent fire from heaven to consume the sacrifice, turning the hearts of the people back to Him. In Daniel 9, Daniel prayed for the restoration of Jerusalem, confessing the sins of the people and pleading with God for mercy. In each of these examples, personal prayer was the catalyst for a greater move of God.

Prayer aligns your heart with God's heart. It draws you into deeper intimacy with Him, and as you spend time in His presence, your heart begins to burn for the things that burn in His heart. Revival starts with this kind of personal prayer—prayer that seeks God's will above all else, prayer that intercedes for the brokenness in the world, and prayer that humbly asks God to bring His Kingdom on earth as it is in heaven.

Worship as a Lifestyle of Revival

Revival is not just about prayer; it is about a lifestyle of worship and surrender. Romans 12:1 teaches us that true worship is offering our bodies as living sacrifices to God, holy and pleasing to Him. Worship is not just something we do in church; it is how we live every day. When your life becomes a living sacrifice, it becomes the spark for revival in others.

Worship as a lifestyle is about surrendering every area of your life to God—your thoughts, your actions, your decisions, your relationships. It is about living in a way that reflects the holiness of God and invites His presence into every moment. When your life is marked by this kind of worship, it creates an atmosphere where God's Spirit can move freely. Worship breaks down the barriers that separate us from God and draws us into deeper intimacy with Him.

Think of King David, a man after God's own heart, who lived a life of worship. His heart was fully devoted to God, and as a result, God's presence dwelled with him. When David brought the Ark of the Covenant back to Jerusalem, he danced before the Lord with all his might, not caring what others thought of him. This kind of abandoned worship invites the presence of God, and where God's presence is, revival follows.

The Role of Obedience in Revival

Revival requires more than just prayer and worship; it requires obedience. When God speaks, revival happens in those who are willing to listen and obey. In 1 Samuel 15:22 (NKJV), the prophet Samuel says, *"To obey is better than sacrifice, and to heed is better than the fat of rams."* Revival begins when we stop doing things our way and start doing things God's way.

Obedience positions you to be part of what God is doing. When the disciples obeyed Jesus' instruction to wait in Jerusalem for the Holy Spirit, they were in the right place at the right time to experience the outpouring of Pentecost. When you walk in obedience to God's Word, you position yourself for revival. Obedience opens the door for God's blessings, for His power to flow through you.

But obedience is not always easy. It requires humility and surrender. It requires laying down your plans, your desires, and even your fears to follow God's lead. But as you walk in obedience, you will begin to see the fruit of revival in your life and in the lives of those around you. Revival starts with individuals who are willing to say "yes" to God, no matter the cost.

Revival in Your Family and Community

When revival begins in your heart, it doesn't stay there. It spreads to your family, your friends, your church, and your community. As you begin to live a life of prayer, worship, and obedience, others will take notice. Your life will become a testimony of God's power and love, and others will be drawn to the fire burning within you.

The exciting thing is that the revival that starts with you can spark a fire in your family. As you pray for your family, live a life of worship before them, and walk in obedience to God, you create an environment where God's presence can move. Just as the Philippian jailer in Acts 16 saw the power of God in Paul and Silas and was saved along with his whole household, so too can revival spread from you to your family.

The revival that starts with you can also spread to your community. When people see the transformation in your life, they will want what you have. Revival is contagious. It is not something that can be contained. Just as the fire of Pentecost spread from the upper room to the streets of Jerusalem, so too can the fire of revival spread from your life to your community. As you live out your faith in front of others, they will be drawn to the God who is alive and at work in you.

Most revivals have very small beginnings, but as they take hold their affect has a ripple effect that can reach far beyond what you can imagine. It starts with you—your heart, your prayers, your worship, your obedience. But as God's Spirit transforms you, the impact of that transformation extends outward. Like a stone thrown into a pond, the ripples of revival spread, touching the lives of those around you.

Consider the story of the woman at the well in John 4. After her encounter with Jesus, she was so transformed that she went back to her village and told everyone about Him. As a result, many in the village came to believe in Jesus. What started with one woman's encounter with Jesus sparked a revival in her community. The same is true for you. Your personal revival can have a far-reaching impact as others see the change in your life and are drawn to Christ.

Revival is something that God wants to start in you today. The call to revival is personal. It is a call to humble yourself before God, to seek His face, to pray, and to turn from anything that hinders your relationship with Him. It's a call to live a life of worship and obedience, trusting that as you do, God will move in and through you.

As we see in 2 Chronicles 7:14, the promise of revival is clear: *"If my people, who are called by my name, will humble themselves and pray and seek my face and turn from their wicked ways, then I will hear from heaven, and I will forgive their sin and will heal their land."* The healing and revival we long for in our land begins with each one of us. It begins as we fully surrender our hearts to God.

Will you answer the call? Will you be the spark that ignites a fire in your family, your church, and your community?

Revival starts with you. It starts with your decision to humble yourself, to pray, to seek God's face, and to live a life of worship and obedience. When you do, you position yourself to be a vessel through which God's Spirit can flow, bringing revival to those around you.

Conclusion: Stay Up Here

Colossians 3:1-2 - "Set your minds on things above, not on earthly things."

We have spent much of this journey exploring what it means to "go up"—to ascend into God's presence, to experience deeper intimacy through prayer and worship, and to embrace the revival that transforms both individuals and communities. But the real challenge begins once you have gone up. What happens next? How do you stay in that place of spiritual vibrancy, where you are continually connected to God, living in the fullness

Colossians 3:1-2 reminds us to *"Set your minds on things above, not on earthly things."* This is a life of abiding, where our hearts and minds are anchored in the things of heaven, even as we walk out our daily lives here on earth. Staying up here requires intentionality, commitment, and a deep desire to remain in God's presence, no matter what distractions or challenges come our way.

Staying up here means living in God's presence as a continual state, not just something we tap into when we feel like it or when we are in crisis. It is about learning to walk with Him in the mundane moments just as much as in the mountaintop experiences. Too often, we treat God like a lifeline, only calling on Him when we are in trouble, instead of making Him the center of our everyday lives.

There is a scripture in John 15:4 where Jesus says, *"Abide in Me, and I in you. As the branch cannot bear fruit of itself unless it abides in the vine, neither can you unless you abide in Me."* Abiding is more than visiting; it is a continual, life-giving connection. It is waking up with the awareness that God is with you, guiding your steps, speaking into your decisions, and filling your heart with His peace. When you make abiding in Him your lifestyle, you will find that His presence is always there, available and ready to sustain you.

When you disconnect from God, you lose the very source of your life and strength. This connection doesn't just happen on Sundays or during morning devotions; it happens moment by moment, through prayer, worship, and intentional focus on God's presence in your life.

But staying connected is not easy. The pull of the world, the busyness of life, and the distractions of our own desires constantly try to drag us down. It's like spiritual gravity, everything around us tries to keep us focused on earthly things, pulling us away from the higher places where God dwells. That is why Paul's instruction to *"set your minds on things above"* is so critical. It is not a one-time decision; it's a daily choice to refocus, realign, and reconnect with God.

Think of it like tuning a radio. You don't just find the right station once and leave it there forever. You must constantly adjust the dial to stay tuned in, because interference and static will always try to distort the signal. Staying spiritually connected works the same way. You have to keep adjusting, keep tuning your heart and mind to the frequency of heaven, no matter what noise is going on around you.

Practical Steps to Stay Up Here

So, how do you stay up here? How do you maintain that connection with God day after day, even when life gets chaotic, and distractions are all around? It starts with creating rhythms of spiritual practice that keep you aligned with His presence.

1. **Cultivate a Daily Prayer Life** – Prayer is your lifeline to God. It is the ongoing conversation that keeps you connected to His heart and His will for your life. Make time for daily prayer, not just in the moments when you need something, but as a regular practice of seeking His face and aligning your heart with His. Let prayer

become as natural as breathing, an ever-present dialogue between you and your Father.

2. **Prioritize Worship** – Worship is more than singing songs, it is a lifestyle of adoration and surrender. Worship shifts your focus from the earthly to the heavenly, reminding you of God's greatness and His nearness. Find moments throughout your day to worship, whether through song, spoken words, or simply in your heart. Worship keeps your heart anchored in His presence.

3. **Stay in the Word** – God's Word is a lamp to our feet and a light to our path (Psalm 119:105). Knowing God's Word will do wonders for your theology. It is through Scripture that we hear God's voice and receive guidance for our lives. Jesus said His sheep know His voice and the voice of a stranger they WILL NOT follow. Make time daily to read and meditate on the Word. Let it renew your mind and shape your perspective, keeping your thoughts focused on things above.

4. **Surround Yourself with Community** – Enlarge your world and you will never be stuck in your own world. Staying up here isn't something you can do alone. We need the support and encouragement of other believers who are also seeking to live in God's presence. Find a community of like-minded people who will challenge you, hold you accountable, and spur you on in your walk with God. Find a tribe that encourages you to share your faith, pray, worship, serve and give sacrificially, because very few who travel alone actually do these things. As Proverbs 27:17 says, *"As iron sharpens iron, so one person sharpens another."*

5. **Guard Your Heart and Mind** – To stay up here, you must protect what enters your heart and mind. Be mindful of the things you consume—whether it is media, conversations, or activities. Philippians 4:8 gives us a clear guide: *"Whatever is true, whatever is noble, whatever is right, whatever is pure, whatever is lovely, whatever is admirable—if anything is excellent or praiseworthy—think about such things."* Stay vigilant about what you allow to shape your thoughts and desires.

Remaining in His Presence Through Trials

Life is full of ups and downs, and staying in God's presence does not mean we won't face difficulties. In fact, it is often in the hardest moments that we need to cling to Him the most. The enemy will try to use trials to pull you away from God, but those are the very moments when you need to press in even deeper. Psalm 23 reminds us that even when we walk through the valley of the shadow of death, we do not need to fear because God is with us.

Staying up here means trusting that God is with you in every situation, even when you don't feel it. It is choosing faith over fear, choosing to believe that God is working all things together for your good, even when the circumstances don't make sense. When trials come, let them drive you closer to God, not further away. Let them remind you of your need for His presence, and press in with prayer, worship, and trust.

The reward for staying up here is more than just a sense of peace or joy, it is the fullness of life that Jesus promised. When you remain connected to God, you begin to bear fruit that lasts. Your life becomes a reflection of His love, His power, and His glory. You become a vessel through which God's Spirit flows, touching the lives of those around you.

In John 15:5, Jesus said, *"I am the vine; you are the branches. If you remain in Me and I in you, you will bear much fruit; apart from Me you can do nothing."* The more you stay connected to God, the more you will see His fruit in your life—love, joy, peace, patience, kindness, goodness, faithfulness, gentleness, and self-control (Galatians 5:22-23). These are the markers of a life that abides in Him.

Staying up here also means living with a heavenly perspective. When your mind is set on things above, you begin to see the world through God's eyes. You see opportunities to love, serve, and bring His Kingdom to earth. You live with purpose, knowing that your life is part of a bigger story, God's story of redemption and restoration.

A Life of Abiding

The invitation to "go up" was never meant to be temporary. It is a call to live in God's presence continually, to make abiding in Him your lifestyle. Colossians 3:2 reminds us to *"Set your minds on things above, not on earthly things,"* because that's where real life is found, in the presence of God.

So, stay up here. Do not settle for brief visits or moments of connection. Make God's presence the center of your life, the place where you dwell every day. Let prayer, worship, and the Word become the foundation of your spiritual life, and you'll find that staying up here is not only possible but life-changing. The rewards are far greater than anything this world could offer, for in His presence is fullness of joy, and at His right hand are pleasures forevermore (Psalm 16:11). Keep your heart and mind set on things above, and watch as God leads you into deeper intimacy, greater purpose, and abundant life.

www.ingramcontent.com/pod-product-compliance
Lightning Source LLC
Chambersburg PA
CBHW061750070526
44585CB00025B/2850